11/1981

THE HEALTHY
ADOLESCENT

Barry Lauton, M.D.
Arthur S. Freese

THE HEALTHY ADOLESCENT

A PARENTS' MANUAL

CHARLES SCRIBNER'S SONS
New York

Copyright © 1981 Barry Lauton, M.D., and Arthur S. Freese

Library of Congress Cataloging in Publication Data

Lauton, Barry.
  The healthy adolescent.

  Bibliography: p.
  Includes index.
  1. Adolescence. 2. Adolescent psychology. 3. Youth—
Care and hygiene. I. Freese, Arthur S., joint author.
II. Title. [DNLM: Adolescent psychology—Popular
works. 2. Parent-child relations—Popular works. WS 462
L389h]
HQ796.L345   305.2'3   80-28031
ISBN 0-684-16819-7   AACR1

This book published simultaneously in the United States of America and in
Canada—Copyright under the Berne Convention.

1 3 5 7 9 11 13 15 17 19 Y/C 20 18 16 14 12 10 8 6 4 2

Printed in the United States of America

Contents

INTRODUCTION

PARENTS of teen-agers today are puzzled and need help. They want to know how their youngsters grow and why they act the way they do; why they are troubled and how they can be helped through the stormy period of adolescence; what their life-styles should be and how they can be protected from overindulgence; what their physical, emotional, and medical problems may be and how they can be treated.

This book is planned to answer these questions. The teen years are a unique period in the human life cycle, and so they must be given special attention. We will examine the psychology of adolescence: how teen-agers act and think, how they develop into adults, and how they face the problems they—and their parents—encounter in the process.

Young people today are experiencing a new rate of growth and development, and this rapid maturation causes a multitude of problems. We will explore these problems and show you how to cope with the unfolding emotional, physical, and mental adjustments teen-agers undergo in their struggle to be themselves.

Parents should look at their complex youngsters in a variety of ways—with humor, with affection, with sympathy, with anger, but never with resentment. How parents react depends largely on their own expectations as teen-agers. Yet, as we discuss in more detail in Chapters 3 and 4, adolescence is so traumatic that very few adults can recall the period and all its suffering. Adults usually remember adolescence in terms of simple events devoid of emotional content.

To compound the problem, the parents of teen-agers are usually in their late thirties, forties, or fifties. Such adults look at life differently from their teen-agers, who grew up during the American sexual and social revolution of recent years. Later on we examine the effects of cultural changes, but before the parents of today's youngsters become too upset by their teen-agers, they should remember what Socrates said centuries ago: "Our youth loves luxury. They have bad manners and contempt for authority. They show disrespect for their elders. . . ." The problems of adolescence haven't changed at all.

Part One

WHAT PARENTS MUST KNOW ABOUT THE TEEN YEARS

One

THE ADOLESCENT

> I would there were no age between ten
> and three-and-twenty, or that youth
> would sleep out the rest; for there is
> nothing in the between but getting
> wenches with child, wronging the
> ancientry, stealing, fighting . . .
>
> *The Winter's Tale*

TEEN-AGERS today have a more positive—and more significant—side than Shakespeare captured in his *Winter's Tale.* One of America's leading authorities on adolescents, Washington University professor of child psychiatry Dr. E. James Anthony, describes adolescence as "the most exciting and energizing and exhilarating (and even exasperating) developmental period in the entire human life cycle. . . . Every other developmental period seems to pale by comparison. . . . Something combustible happens at the time of adolescence when the repetition of all that was converges on the rehearsal of what is to come in the adolescent's 'now,' giving it an intensity that will never be experienced again."

How does the parent deal with the strange but never-boring adolescent? One Chicago suburban couple recall their fourteen-year-old daughter's shrieking at them: "I'm not going to do anything just because you want me to—

and there isn't a damn thing you can do about it!" A Seattle father reports that his sixteen-year-old son blurted: "I won't mow that lawn or help you with those storm windows; in fact, you can go straight to hell!" Yet even these parents—most parents, in fact—remember moments of tenderness and times when their teen-ager was kind and thoughtful and helpful. Parents should perhaps keep in mind this apt description of the teen-ager: a person who acts like a child unless treated like an adult.

Despite the fury of the storm for many teen-agers, adolescence remains a miracle of human growth and development. The teen years are second only to the first six to twelve months of life in terms of physical change and accelerated growth. The confusion accompanying any period of biological change is particularly evident in teen-agers, since their emotions can shift as quickly as the color patterns in a kaleidoscope. Teen-agers and parents pay dearly in pain and turmoil for that biological miracle of growth during which the child is changed into the adult.

The teen years are a bewildering period for children, who feel uncomfortable with themselves as they struggle to. develop new personalities in the midst of internal hormonal changes and new external social responsibilities. It's not surprising that a teen-ager behaves like an adult one moment and a child the next, sometimes simultaneously within a single conversation.

But somehow, thanks to nature, all the problems work out—the adolescent becomes an adult, emotional storms subside, and a mature calm replaces the adolescent's conflicts. Finally, too, the rebelliousness characteristic of some teen-agers fades away as they establish their own identities. Once teen-agers discover that they really are independent, they no longer need to keep their fists up whenever you approach them. But in the end, the joys and the burdens of this nearly decade-long journey belong to the parents to savor and bear.

WHAT IS ADOLESCENCE?

Adolescence is often called the in-between years or the awkward age. Such terms are misleading, because they deceive adults into thinking of adolescence as an interlude, a marking of time, as it were, between the more important periods of childhood and adulthood. It must not be forgotten that adolescents are in the process of becoming young adults capable of actively contributing to the world in which they live.

To understand adolescence fully we must see it as a process and not as any one specific event in time. Understanding adolescence is similar to understanding the creation of a new human being, for the ultimate result of adolescence is adulthood, and its process is comparable to the nine-month period of gestation. New life grows in the uterus slowly until the infant is ready to be born. Although birth itself adds a new human being to a family at a specific time, birth is only the culmination of a long process of development. Similarly, the adolescent becomes a man or woman, a mature adult, gradually and painstakingly, even though in retrospect a child seems to grow up all too fast.

As if to emphasize the complex and multidimensional aspects of adolescence, the term itself covers both process and period. Dictionaries recognize this duality; the *Oxford English Dictionary*, for example, begins its definition with the word *process*. The word *adolescent*, used in our language for almost six hundred years, derives from the Latin *adolescere*, meaning "to grow up."

Adolescence actually begins with puberty (the stage of sexual development when the child becomes functionally capable of reproduction) and concludes with adulthood. For a variety of reasons, it is impossible to pinpoint the exact age range of adolescence. All children mature at individual rates—which vary widely, with no regard for what doctors or textbooks say. As we discuss in Chapter 4, the average age at which puberty begins has been modified: it now starts earlier than ever before in the history of human development.

Most cultures and societies have recognized puberty as an important event. Furthermore, the end of adolescence and the advent of full maturity is usually marked by a variety of rights and responsibilities, the attributes and privileges of adulthood. In our own society such privileges include voting, drinking, and driving. The ages at which these privileges are conferred vary, and they are constantly reevaluated as modern life turns adolescents into young adults more quickly than ever before. However, physical and emotional maturity do not always coincide; emotional development occurs more slowly than physical maturation. In general, adolescence has traditionally been regarded as the teen years, although today adolescence actually starts around ten to twelve years of age.

Next we see what nature demands of burgeoning adolescents as they alter and grow.

Two

ADOLESCENCE:
ITS PHASES AND GOALS

A child's growth is only a subtle indication of the many physical and emotional phases a young body undergoes. Temperamental outbursts manifest these changes and result in the tense moments of growing up, yet youngsters do work out the crises that seem to come hand in hand with adolescence. As your children stumble into adulthood, they will develop new patterns of thinking and of behavior. Your help and support are important at this stage. You cannot share your child's growing pains, but you can lessen the anguish with understanding.

WHAT HAPPENS
DURING THE TEEN YEARS

The thrilling metamorphosis that takes place during adolescence, called maturation, involves physical, sexual, psychological, and social changes. Along with the changes, each phase of growing up brings with it certain behavior patterns. Every stage of life—childhood, adolescence, early adulthood, middle age, and old age—has its own patterns. Growth patterns are biologically programmed into the human being from the very moment of conception, but while nature has made reproduction and survival the basic aims of all life, humanity has subverted and enlarged these automatic goals. Humanity has raised its sights and set the typically human values—love, creativity, altruism, desire to improve society, and even life itself—above nature's own primitive biological drives.

For a confused adolescent, the erratic behavior brought about by biological changes can be mind-blowing. Some youngsters become emotionally distraught. Since teenagers experience change inside and out—in bodily proportions and looks, in hormonal and biochemical composition, in sexual, psychological, and social urges and capacities—it is a miracle that almost all young people succeed in passing through the storminess and confusion of this period with triumph.

The emotional changes of adolescence that differentiate it from other human stages of development, according to the renowned psychotherapist Erik Erikson, are a crystallization or consolidation of identity. The ultimate attainment of identity during this stage, which is the primary emotional goal of adolescence, occurs when the teen-ager truly understands himself and when his ideas about himself and others can comfortably coexist. Teen-agers who feel threatened by others have yet to establish their own identities and may suffer an "identity crisis."

Caused by uncertainty, an identity crisis results in a reexamination of all one's most fundamental values—one's choice of career, one's approach and attitude toward life, one's belief in what is good or bad, one's religion, one's sense of self-worth. The individual suffering from an identity crisis often cannot focus his energies and may have to take time out from the business of living in order to let his thinking—his soul if you will—catch up with his body. Often, a good relationship with parents will prevent an identity crisis of serious proportions. On the other hand, when the relationship is insecure or weak, the likelihood of a crisis of this sort is much greater.

PHASES AND GOALS

Those who deal professionally with teen-agers distinguish the phases of adolescence to accord with the goals that adolescents must attain during each stage. The most acceptable division breaks up adolescence into early, middle, and late periods—each having its own special goals, changes, and adjustments. Each phase must be successfully negotiated by the youngster so that he can move into the next stage and eventually reach mature adulthood.

Early Adolescence

Early adolescence comprises the years from eleven to thirteen in girls and twelve to fourteen in boys. The goal is to deal with puberty: the child is faced with the need to cope with growing sexual development and awareness, along with the physical and emotional changes that result from increased sex hormones and glandular activity.

Although we will leave the details for Chapter 4, let's look now at a general time frame for the physical and sexual changes to occur. Adolescent girls grow fastest around the ages of twelve or thirteen, shortly before menarche (the onset of menstruation). In boys the most rapid growth spurt is less easily predicted; it usually occurs one to two years after the first changes of puberty appear— roughly around the ages of thirteen or fourteen. But the phases of growth are really quite vague and merge into each other almost imperceptibly. Distinct differences, however, do exist between the stages, and each stage varies among individual adolescents.

Adolescent goals—conscious or not—include establishing identity, giving up dependency, becoming emancipated from parents, choosing a career, and developing a commitment to responsible citizenship and to a particular role and place in society. Young people must determine and settle upon the value system and personal standards by which they will live the rest of their lives. In addition, teen-agers also have to learn how to deal maturely with authority—the parent and the teacher, the employer or the superior on the job, and the laws of society. Moreover, teen-agers must develop comfortable feelings about themselves in terms of their own competence in order to gain self-esteem.

It is difficult to appreciate fully the extent and the complexity of the tasks that youngsters must struggle with and accomplish in a few years—often without knowing what is expected of them. Their efforts can be obstructed or simplified by their environment and by their parents. Teachers, doctors, coaches, and other adults can also help or hinder a youngster's efforts to grow up.

Culture plays a powerful role in adolescent behavior as well. Our social barriers inhibit early sexual involvement between boys and girls and keep them relatively separate through childhood and early adolescence. As a result, we don't see much one-on-one expression of sexual feelings, interests, and involvement. Instead, a group of girls will tease or heckle a group of boys, or the boys will pick on the girls. Games are particularly useful for bringing boys and girls together. The pushing or shoving, the general rough-housing that goes on during play, establish physical contact and release some tension.

Since girls mature earlier than boys, they are likely to be bigger and stronger in early adolescence and so are more likely to be the aggressors at this stage. Although this kind of physical activity may not be enough to satisfy the sexual drives of some of these children, our social taboos have generally proven sufficient to prevent sexual relationships at an early age. It is to replace sexual drives that intense friendships with someone of the same sex arise. Parents should tolerate the inseparability of two youngsters of the same age and sex—their interminable telephone conversations and their desire to do everything together.

Today menarche begins earlier than ever before, and most girls, forewarned by their mothers or teachers, are prepared for menstruation. But in our society boys usually aren't so well informed, and so their early seminal ejaculations ("wet dreams") can be confusing and frightening, causing young boys to withdraw in shame. Because of these changes, youngsters often lose interest in their schoolwork; junior high school teachers are frequently aware of a drop-off in the quality of their seventh- and eighth-graders' work. Parents may notice sudden outbreaks of shyness, irritability, or even various psychosomatic symptoms such as headaches and vague abdominal pains and fatigue.

Besides all the difficulties of learning how to deal with new and unaccustomed sexual sensations, the young teen-ager also has to learn to fit himself into an entirely new body, one that is uncomfortably large. Adolescents usually reach full height by seventeen or eighteen years of age, although body size may continue to increase because of muscular development. During adolescence the body needs more calories, vitamins, and minerals than at any other time. That's why normal teen-agers seem to eat so ravenously. Sexual changes begin in girls about two years earlier than in boys, and such early development leads to marked social complications among children. The first signs of puberty in girls are breast development, the appearance of pubic hair, and, of course, menstruation. In boys the most obvious early sexual changes involve genital organ size and the ability to ejaculate. However, a girl is not sexually mature simply because she has begun to menstruate or a boy because he has become capable of ejaculation. The maximal development of the sexual organs in both sexes is reached at about the time the adolescent attains full adult height.

The age at which adolescent growth and development begins is highly variable and individual: teen-agers mature at different rates. Sexual, psychological, and social development each march to the beat of different drums. Parents are often misled by their teen-ager's physical size into thinking the child is more psychologically mature than he actually is. Guard against such wishful thinking.

The uneven growth rate makes life difficult for youngsters, since friends often find themselves at different stages of development. Such physical discrepancies compound the teen-ager's already considerable problems. Youngsters can be painfully sensitive about their physical characteristics. They are very aware of and easily disturbed by any deviation from what they consider to be the "normal" size or shape either of the body as a whole or of any part. Somehow, growing boys and girls have to adjust to their big, strange bodies, a process that inspires the term "the awkward age." The awkwardness is simply the result of the difficulty of learning to manipulate and operate their new physiques.

Middle Adolescence

Middle adolescence, usually the most difficult time for teen-agers, spans the years thirteen to sixteen in girls and fourteen to seventeen in boys. Teen-agers at this stage tend to pull away from their parents in a desire for independence. Family harmony depends on whether the parents try to aid or to frustrate their child's drive for independence (a problem we will explore in detail in the next chapter). In this period of adolescent ambivalence, the swings from "yes" to "no," from dependence to independence, become most marked, with violent oscillations in emotions and behavior. Parents and child alike strain to deal with the youngster's erratic and abrupt changes in feelings, interests, and behavior, all part of the underlying struggle of growth.

Concern about their appearance intensifies at this time to further plague most adolescents and their parents. Youngsters become preoccupied with their skin and hair, their eyeglasses and clothes, height and weight. (One desperate parent threatened to take the mirror door off the medicine chest to get his sixteen-year-old son out of the bathroom.) This stage frequently produces spells of cleanliness alternating with bouts of dishevelment. This pattern may be an expression of conflict within the teen-ager or may simply be a test to see how effective some particular behavior is in upsetting the parents.

Sexually, this is a difficult time, and most teen-agers masturbate to relieve sexual drives if such activities as dancing or athletics don't dissipate the tension.

Many teen-agers vacillate between considerate behavior and insulting rudeness; a particular phase can last for an hour or a day or many weeks—and be reversed without warning. It's a head-spinning time for those concerned, and parents must show a great deal of compassion, love, and understanding, along with a good sense of humor.

Late Adolescence

Late adolescence is the final phase, the years after sixteen and seventeen. During this period adolescents establish their values. They grow up.

Emotional maturity is a tall order, an awesome responsibility for young people, but their parents combined probably have nearly half a century of knowledge and experience with which to help their sons and daughters. Unfortunately, it is difficult for many teen-agers to accept their parents' advice, because they want to seem independent; they want to be able to cope on their own. Ultimately, a teen-ager's independent spirit will make possible a new relationship in which the accumulated wisdom of the adults will be recognized and appreciated.

An adolescent's main goal is to establish an identity separate from that of his parents. When the teen-ager fails to be satisfied with himself, he may suffer an identity crisis and question first his values and beliefs, then his family's, and finally society's. Such a youngster will reexamine all his own basic choices, his life-style, and his approach to life. The teen-agers who have the strength and the aggressive energy to persevere will succeed in "finding themselves." If their parental relationships are solid, their parents can provide vital help and support at this crucial time. Both the teen-ager and the parent must be willing to communicate with each other to avoid the pitfalls of adolescent isolation.

It is among the relatively few teen-agers who undergo an identity crisis that we often find "revolutionaries" and those who become involved with drugs. The young people who develop a "negative identity" tend to rebel against themselves and all those with whom they should have satisfying relationships. The hostile, angry teen-ager who feels left out reacts self-destructively and needs special help.

Most young people manage to find their way successfully sooner or later—and how exciting they are as a group, how valuable and creative their challenges to society can be! They can raise the level of society once they have established a position for themselves. One can only regret that nature has sometimes made the emotional price of growth so high for both parent and child.

BEHAVIORAL PROBLEMS

All stages of life should encourage growth and change. The teen-ager changes the most dramatically and must come to terms with the excitement and the inevitable force that drives him to grow whether he wills it or not.

The path from adolescence to adulthood does not allow an orderly progression, for it is an erratic emotional passage—neither smooth, steady, nor even. Rather it is one of unpredictable stops and starts. Teen-agers want to be treated as adults one moment, and yet they continue to act like children. They're not sure if they are ready to accept the responsibilities of adulthood, but they certainly want its pleasures and privileges. Most parents do enjoy their teen-agers—when their deliberate baiting doesn't make the most phlegmatic of parents explode.

Satisfy the interests and curiosities of a teen-ager and he may progress at a startling pace, but thwart him and he may not be able to control his anger. Adolescents often find great comfort and support in striving to be like their peers, and so they may seem to reject their parents and other adults. This attitude is reinforced by the mass media, which suggest that youngsters should look alike, behave alike, eat the same foods, and wear the same clothes in order to be acceptable. Today's teen-ager has a good deal more freedom than ever before, and he may think it allows him to act in new and bizarre ways. He may behave in ways that startle or frighten or defy his parents. As one child told his father when he was being disciplined: "I'm the boss of myself."

The transition from dependence to independence, from childhood to maturity, has never been easy, and it is made even harder in the disturbed world of today; in fact, the concern over the relative ease with which we can all be blown to kingdom come with a few hydrogen bombs frightens most adolescents (whose own control is, at best, uncertain). An awareness of the vulnerability of the world in which they live increases their insecurity and promotes disillusionment.

Unsure of himself and of what others think of him, a teen-ager will often test the esteem in which he is held by behaving badly simply to make sure that he is loved no matter how he behaves. Demonstrate your love at all times and help placate your teen-ager's fears.

Sometimes a teen-ager's behavior reveals serious emotional problems. Recognizing emotional illness isn't easy, so we'll examine this in more detail in Chapter 13. Just remember that teen-agers can be emotionally unstable: suicide is the most common cause of death among college youths today. Its increase among youngsters will be discussed in Chapter 14.

Some teen-agers are emotionally maladjusted and indulge in what is called acting-out behavior. They deal with their emotional difficulties by stealing, driving at high speeds, causing trouble at school or on the job, abusing drugs, and engaging in other activities that cause their usefulness to be impaired and their future to be imperiled. The symptoms of maladjustment are sometimes more subtle, such as restlessness, anxiety, tension, sleeplessness, prolonged solitude, lack of friends, headaches, intestinal upsets, depression, delusion, hallucinations, paranoid thinking, and so on. These symptoms indicate a need to consult a physician to discover if underlying physical causes do exist.

Sexual promiscuity can be a form of acting-out behavior, especially for girls, since most societies more readily tolerate indiscriminate sexual activity among boys. Homosexual relationships may occur when the introduction to heterosexual activity has been distressful or aberrant. Sex education is the best way to prepare your child for sexual experience. Ignorance causes needless anxiety.

The possibilities inherent in freedom of choice tend to confuse rather than free the adolescent. Alienation, anger, bitterness, resentment, and defiance may result from numerous experiences that are ambiguous or discouraging. Alienated youngsters are more likely to listen to each other than to pay attention to what they hear from adults, who they think are past the point of understanding. Be patient: always try to understand your child's point of view, but let him learn from his mistakes.

Some adolescents are quite capable of becoming involved in working to solve their problems and society's. The opportunity to confront social problems in their community by visiting places such as homes for the aged may increase a teen-ager's confidence and self-esteem. Many teen-agers can be helpful if given the chance to show that they care.

THE FINAL GOAL: EMOTIONAL MATURITY

The final goal of adolescence is emotional maturity, which takes longer to develop than biological, physical, or sexual maturity. An emotionally mature person can deal reasonably, effectively, and responsibly with the demands of the world about him, he can learn from his experiences, and he can relate to others in a satisfactory way in work, in play, and in love. Maturity and mental health have much in common, for both are found in people with thoughtful, sincere, humane attitudes, people who are concerned for others and willing to modify their behavior to suit the situation. Many teen-agers are capable of emotional maturity and social responsibility.

Much of the suffering that parents and teen-agers undergo is reflected in their relationships. The next two chapters are devoted to this difficult and delicate problem and to the ways in which parent–child relationships can be improved.

Three

THE GENERATION GAP: A PERPETUAL STRUGGLE

A mother told us: "I'm terrified of next year when my boy will be thirteen. The beginning of the teens—everybody knows what that means!"

Many parents of preteen-agers feel they have to gear themselves up emotionally in anticipation of the worst struggle of their lives; they inevitably worry about the generation gap and its conflicts. The existence of a struggle between parent and child may seem ironic, given the similar genes and the nurturing that parents give their children during the early years, but strife often does arise, and it is a fact of life most parents must accept.

Just as the adolescent struggles with the problems of youth, so do parents struggle with problems of age. The latter are nearing middle age, which, like the teen years, is a difficult period full of its own crises, requiring insight and understanding to resolve.

Superficially it may seem odd that parents—who have

already passed through adolescence—do not have a greater tolerance for its troubles. But if you consider the severe adolescent problems—trauma, confusion, guilt, anger, depression—that are too often the hallmarks of this period, it becomes easy to understand why many adults don't remember. It's what psychiatrists call denial: adults forget their teen years, or remember the events without the emotions tied to them, or clothe the time in a rosy robe and recall everything that happened as fun and games with no memory of the pain, confusion, and suffering.

Dr. Beverly T. Mead, a Creighton University professor of psychiatry, warns that "the generation gap is likely to become a national landmark as firmly entrenched as the Royal Gorge unless more constructive approaches to parent–child relationships are developed." Dr. Seymour L. Halleck, a professor of psychiatry at the University of North Carolina, warns of the resentment and hostility felt toward adolescents by adults over thirty. Dr. Halleck finds that few adults deal with their own feelings honestly, face their own ambivalences, or reveal their anger to the young. The result is devastating to young and old alike, for the teen-ager fails to gain the necessary awareness of how others objectively regard his behavior. Furthermore, the teen-ager may recognize the anger and become more distrustful of adults. So difficult is adolescence in general that emotional problems may never be resolved, and so many adults react to their own adolescents just as their parents did. Repressing the pain and torment of their own youth makes it more difficult for adults to deal with the teen-ager whose experiences stir up buried memories of the past.

Other studies reveal that despite tension and anger, deep ties of love and respect may exist between teen-agers and their parents. Adolescence is undeniably a time of inter-generational strife, but a patient and knowledgeable parent can turn the situation to advantage so that, regardless of the turmoil, new and stronger ties can be formed for the inevitable day when the child becomes an adult and leaves home.

Parents have a double load to bear in the monumental task of allowing a child to develop independence: they must deal first with their own problems, and then with those of their children. It takes strong and mature parents to cope with adolescents. As their children grow up, parents must continuously offer support and advice and supply the benefits of their own experience, knowledge, and material resources, even though some teen-agers may sneer at all their parents offer. Parents must smooth the way and help youngsters with the problems of becoming independent even at the cost of the emotional pain caused by the separation. Patient parents will eventually gain a lifelong adult and rewarding relationship with their sons and daughters.

Everybody needs to be loved and respected, to have self-esteem. As adolescents today gain increasing knowledge, they often see defects in their parents' values and ruthlessly attack them. Some teen-agers may cold-bloodedly point out their parents' inadequacies. A middle-aged father, already painfully aware of rapidly becoming obsolete in his job, feels he can no longer keep pace with all the new developments that today can make even adults in their early thirties outdated. Middle-aged adults are especially exposed and sensitive to sneering children who denounce their parents' material accomplishments and their struggle to live dignified lives.

It is obvious that the admired person in our society today is the young one. Business caters to the youth market, and industry looks for ever-younger employees. The middle-aged man or woman often cannot find jobs or suitable clothes, for these, like music, advertising, and hair styles, are geared to the young. This bias emphasizes the identity crisis that has always troubled and isolated the middle aged. But, as Dr. Halleck points out, those of us in the older age group must come to terms with our anger toward the young. We must not feel unwanted: we can render a valuable service to young people. Parents who fight back against a new life-style by using family, business, or school pressure to force their children to conform to the patterns and values of their own youth will only alienate their children. Such rigidity prevents a meeting of the minds, a sharing of experience. Adults must learn to understand what teen-agers themselves are feeling.

THE ADOLESCENT SIDE

The last chapter explored how an adolescent ticks. Certainly it would be nice for all concerned if teen-agers could mature without having to suffer through a torment-ing period, but that cannot be. Children must separate from parents, and it is first the loosening and then severing of parental bonds that is so traumatic for both parents and children. To compound the problem, the internal biochemical and hormonal changes and the need to get comfortable in a new and bigger body frighten many teen-agers. Furthermore, adolescents are totally immersed in the here and now; they have little experience by which they can critically view themselves and evaluate their feelings or those of others. Teen-agers must compress an enormous amount of growth and change into a relatively short period, and the process itself is unsettling.

Youngsters may feel guilt at wanting to be separate from their parents and fearful at leaving their dependent, protected relationship for a totally new and unknown independent existence. Nevertheless, the biological and psychological need to grow drives the adolescent on. One sixteen-year-old boy told his parents, "I don't care what you think, I'm not going to college!" even though he wanted his parents to insist on it. By speaking out, however, he showed he could make up his own mind, be grown up and independent. A seventeen-year-old Los Angeles girl exclaimed, "I can't stand the stifling reaction-ary crap around here"—even though her parents were well known for their long-standing liberalism.

Both youngsters may have been out of contact with reality, but that's part of the way human beings seem to need to grow up. The result is that these teen-agers do grow and mature. Although adults have learned to deal with life's situations in rational and mature terms, teen-agers may react and behave emotionally in ways that may seem bizarre and upsetting to their elders. Teen-agers act childishly because they are still children, despite their seeming carefree and assured surfaces and adult-sized bodies.

Dr. Edwin Z. Levy, child psychiatrist in the Menninger Clinic's children's division, sums up the problem by saying, "Adolescents are sensitive, mercurial, erratic, somewhat irrational and never to be fully comprehended. . . ." The uncertain parent who feels he doesn't fully understand what's going on with his youngster need not feel inadequate—parental confusion is very human and normal. Most parents err in thinking they should be more competent and comprehending. When teen-agers angrily accuse their parents of not understanding them, they may be right, to a degree, but no adult should keep from trying. All teen-agers need parents or other adults to help them in their own bumbling attempts to understand themselves.

A cocksure and insulting attitude may conceal healthy psychic turmoil. It's a rare teen-ager who hasn't told his parents "I won't be bossed" or "I want to be me" in the struggle to find and assume his own identity. Teen-agers often seek self-determination in seemingly outlandish and defiant ways—and concerned parents can only hope it doesn't lead their offspring into irreversible problems in the process. Defiance outside the family—with teachers or prospective employers or school officials—may lead to serious and permanent setbacks. Adults accustomed to dealing with adolescents will often have enough expertise and insight to recognize the symptoms of rebellion and to judge the teen-ager accordingly. Teachers or other school authorities are in a position to exert considerable influence on teen-agers. They may, for example, be able to demonstrate how rebellious behavior is self-defeating and inappropriate. And they may be able to explain to parents that some teen-agers get poor grades to show their independence of excessive pressure, or that others cut classes to show they aren't going to do things just because adults want them to. People used to working with teen-agers can often offer guidance for a troubled family.

Teen-agers want and need privacy. It's important for them to have their own rooms and possessions, their own private thoughts, their mail, phone calls, and diaries untouched by others. Intrusions incite anger, insults, and complaints, which is why "get off my case" or "stop bugging me" are the most frequent and furious refrains of adolescents. Teen-agers want to choose their own friends and their own clothes and take their own chances. Parents need to withstand their children's adventuresomeness bravely and to watch over them with as little interference as possible.

Teen-agers must be given room in which to grow, even at the expense of parental protection. Remember that no parent owns his child—parents only have a responsibility for the temporary custody of a young human being who embodies the most wonderful and exciting aspect of life— potential.

Teen-agers need to know how to give and receive affection; they need to feel needed and wanted, recognized as unique and separate persons, distinct from parents and siblings and not just an extension of them. They need to be free of excessive or unnecessary parental domination and interference in their personal affairs, but they also need firm discipline administered in a friendly and loving way by respected and respectful adults.

Any divided or conflicting authority is especially con- fusing to young people. A specific value system is necessary for the adolescent either to follow or to rebel against. Ethical or moral relativism is particularly damaging to a teen-ager seeking to determine definite and fixed limits, to learn what he can and cannot get away with. The most important service parents can provide is to help their youngsters develop their own goals and limits. If a teen-ager doesn't have sufficient parental or other outside controls to start with, he will suffer great difficulties in fashioning his own inner controls. Discipline will take hold much more rapidly and earlier in life if the reasons for it are explained and if teen-agers are made partners in forming the rules of conduct by which they are expected to live.

PARENTAL AUTHORITY

The often strange or perverse behavior of adolescents today—their raucous music, provocative dress, disturbing sexual promiscuity—produces a smoke screen behind which the real teen-ager frequently hides. The life-styles and views of teen-agers are changing worldwide, and the trends can be confusing to keep pace with. The news media in general and television in particular show the adolescent what teen-agers around the world are doing. Since teen-agers have a tendency to follow their peers, this exposure makes young people imitate any pattern of behavior they come across. Teen-agers conform to the behavior of their peers because they want to be "with it." The standardized but generally unruly conduct of teen-agers today makes discipline the biggest problem parents face.

A teen-ager who stays out late or demands his own car is attempting to prove that he is no longer a child, but parents must not abdicate their authority to their self-styled "adult" children. Parents who treat their children like adults too soon often create insecurity in their youngsters and impose a burden too great to bear. Parents who try to be pals with their children also do a disservice; their sons and daughters may want parental authority, and they may be secretly relieved to have parents who can firmly but lovingly say "no" and thereby save them from making decisions they do not have the experience to handle.

On the other hand, flat edicts based on outdated beliefs rather than on rational judgment often invite defiance. Parents must know when to be firm and when to relax their authority; they must set priorities and stick by them. They must delegate decision making gradually so that the teen-ager will get the feel of the responsibility of taking over his own management—and of learning to rectify his mistakes. It's essential—and most difficult—to get teen-agers into the habit of looking at the possible future results of present actions, but teen-agers must learn to weigh possibilities. They must be willing to accept the price they have to pay for their mistakes, although no punishment or atonement should be unduly severe. Trial and error helps teen-agers make mature decisions and become independent, thoughtful adults.

Freedom of choice and self-discipline are tough control problems to leave to the immature teen-ager. Parents must provide guidance and decide at what age their children are capable of determining policy for themselves. In one suburban Connecticut family, for example, the parents make most of the decisions that are likely to produce permanent effects on their teen-agers. These decisions cover health care, personal safety, school, and career matters. The teen-agers are expected to obey the rules of society and school. They are unobtrusively but firmly supervised. Gradually, though, the parents turn over to their growing youngsters minor matters: the choice of everyday clothes (for serious family discussions or important interviews democratic discussion is held, but the final decision lies with the parents); the choice of elective courses and of friends are left up to the teen-agers. The parents delegate more and more responsibility to the youngsters as they prove equal to the task of caring for themselves.

HOW TO IMPROVE RAPPORT

The combination of troubled adolescent and strict parent makes an explosive situation. Trouble arises when parents force outdated concepts on their children, or when they try to be pals with their children by behaving like teen-agers themselves. Children do not need a peer for a parent; they need a mature adult.

As parents, listening to what your adolescents say and showing respect for their thoughts and feelings is vital—as is letting them know that it's all right to be different from you. Teen-agers must learn that something new isn't inherently good, or that something old isn't bad just because it's been around for a while. Teen-agers must recognize that *old-fashioned* is not synonymous with *worthless* or *irrelevant*. A joint family examination of thinking and beliefs helps determine values, and the practice of openly admitting mistakes helps show that honest error is forgivable and not necessarily catastrophic. An aware parent knows when it's time to exercise authority and set limits, but if restraints are arbitrary, teen-agers will rebel.

Parents must take their teen-agers' problems seriously and try to spend time discussing them. Parents should not simply argue with their children; rather they should compare opinions, supporting their teen-agers by helping them make up their own minds. This may entail time-consuming discussion with thoughtful explanations of the reasons for particular rules, regulations, or modes of behavior. Even if parents feel it is necessary to withhold approval, they should never withhold interest or love. Love must be expressed continuously even when there are sharp clashes.

Adolescents are most likely to respond favorably when their parents have listened attentively to their points of view and have tried carefully to understand them. The teen-ager may be right, and parents must be prepared to recognize this possibility. But even when the parents disagree with their teen-ager's faulty thinking, they should make it clear that they do so with regard only to a particular point.

Adolescents and parents are inextricably linked, and for successful passage through this painful and trying period the teen-ager needs mature parents—in fact, everyone in the family must play his or her role fully and responsibly.

We can only marvel at the success with which so many parents, despite the odds, play their roles in ways that make it possible for teen-agers to achieve happy adulthood. It may be difficult, but it is possible. Some parents, however, cannot control their resentment, and this hostility leads to problems of a very serious nature.

THE ABUSED ADOLESCENT

Professionals interested in adolescents as well as those involved with child abuse are concerned with the millions of teen-agers who suffer physical violence every year in their own homes. In reported cases of child abuse studied from January 1974 to September 1976 in Connecticut, Montana, Arizona, and Maryland, those involving adolescents made up between 24 and 49 percent of the various state reports. In an unpublished paper presented to the American Association for the Advancement of Science by Dr. M. A. Straus and others in Boston in 1976, it was reported that 58 percent of 285 college freshmen interviewed had been struck by their parents the year before they entered college, and 6 percent had received significant injury.

Dr. Reginald Lourie, Deputy Chief of the Center for Studies of Child and Family Mental Health at the National Institute of Mental Health, has found a high percentage of unreported abused adolescents in "runaway" houses. This NIMH expert sees adolescent abuse as a family reaction to the changes that occur in the course of the teen-ager's working out his developmental tasks. In particular, the separation that occurs in this period leads to family violence, as does the provocative behavior of the child in his struggle for freedom and adulthood. These normal behaviors can and do disrupt the family and create so much additional stress that it can spill over into violence against the teen-ager. After all, adolescents can, as Dr. Lourie explains, "tap in on the hidden violence in even the most outwardly gentle parent." One fifteen-year-old youngster in a Boston apartment wanted to open his bedroom window—in opposition to the family health attitudes and beliefs. When the boy insisted, his father chased him around the room, lashing him with his belt and buckle.

Abuse may cause a teen-ager to run away, although some teen-agers, quite capable of either fighting back or of running, will accept the violence passively because of fear and weakened ego defenses. The longer they accept abuse, the harder it is to resist it.

The emotional turbulence resulting from a child's growing older interferes with a parent's ability to cope. Parents who were themselves abused as children are most likely to abuse their own children. When parents use violence as a means of expression, they—as well as their children—need professional counseling.

WHAT TEEN-AGERS
FEEL ABOUT THEIR PARENTS

A young child looks at his parents as all-powerful, all-wise, and all-understanding. During adolescence, the teen-ager sees his parents quite differently, though no more accurately. With breathtaking rapidity, a teen-ager can regard his parents as wondrous wise one moment and as incapable of human comprehension the next. One father related how on Monday his sixteen-year-old daughter told him, "Dad, you're wonderful," and on Tuesday, "You're stupidly old-fashioned—you just don't know anything." However, as the teen years pass, parents are more or less seen to be the ordinary human beings they are, the way they will eventually be recognized and respected by an adult son or daughter.

Teen-agers' attitudes toward their parents today do not differ from those of earlier generations. The children of immigrant parents often looked down on their mothers and fathers and their inability to be "American" or to understand the culture of their new society. Today's parents are also, in a way, strangers in a foreign land. Our current society has changed so radically from the society of even the recent past that parents and their teen-age children often do not speak the same language.

The present adolescent has grown up in a world of hydrogen bombs, lasers, new mathematics, and a science explosion unparalleled in human history. Only in the last decade or two have language, life-styles, methods of communication, and education changed so vastly that parents have become aliens in their own world. The result is that current adolescents—like earlier generations—look with contempt on their parents' inability to adopt or accept society's changes. The reasons for parent/child disaffection may differ from generation to generation, but the existence of differences recurs.

Most young people are not mature enough to recognize

that they still lack the overall wisdom of an adult—even one who can't repair a motorcycle or accept cohabitation instead of marriage. In short, the inexperienced adolescent simply confuses parental limitations in coping with specific aspects of our culture with overall intellectual inadequacy.

But studies belie much of the apparent hostility between parents and teen-agers. Professors Gisela Konopka and Ruth Tester of the University of Minnesota's Center for Youth Development and Research recently interviewed some thousand adolescent girls living in urban and rural areas of the United States who represented a broad range of social, ethnic, and economic backgrounds, ranging from institutions for the delinquent to protected middle-class homes. The researchers reported that "one of the outstanding findings of our recent study of adolescent young women was . . . the importance of adults in their lives. . . . The majority liked adults and admired adults who could understand, listen, be helpful; and they respected the wisdom and experience of such adults." The professors also found a yearning among these teen-agers for adults other than their parents whom they could approach and talk things over with objectively.

This study indicates that all adults must strive to understand what teen-agers are really trying to express in deed and word. One Midwestern thirteen-year-old boy caused trouble at school simply to gain attention from a busy traveling-executive father and a socially active mother. This youngster equated love with attention, and when his parents spent a little more time with him, the problem disappeared. Human communication is never easy, and much of it is nonverbal. Parents must be alerted to all the signs children give in order to discover how they can best respond to their child's needs.

A recent study of Mormon junior high school students found that these teen-agers also looked at their parents in generally positive ways. Many studies, in fact, reveal the strong influence adults actually have on the attitudes, beliefs, and self-images of adolescents—despite all the grief that teen-agers give adults. One study found that the adolescents rated their parents consistently higher than the parents rated themselves. The teen-agers' descriptions of themselves tended to agree with the way their parents rated them. The teen-agers, however, expected their parents to underrate them, and the parents anticipated that their children would overrate their own maturity and ability. Perhaps parents are unfair to themselves when they fail to recognize their own general competence in the difficult problem of parent–teen-ager relationships. And perhaps parents might realize from this study how important it is to convey their love to their children.

Teen-age behavior is due to what Dr. Beverly Mead points out as a youngster's need: "The whole point of adolescence is to outgrow dependent, child-like relationships and learn to be relatively independent. . . . Translated into today's jargon, that means 'learning to cope.'"

THE GENERATION GAP YESTERDAY AND TODAY

No evidence supports the theory that adolescents throughout the ages have differed in their needs or in their capacity to react to social influences. Certainly mankind's physical and hormonal makeup and development have changed only slightly over the centuries. But what does change at a dizzying pace is the world in which human beings live. Our environment is more stimulating and accessible to today's adolescent than it was to previous generations. Young people today, particularly in affluent families, have relatively few demands or responsibilities placed on them at home; they live comfortably with an excess of leisure time. They are constantly brought into contact with the rest of the world through TV sets; they know what is going on, and they react to it. During the past several decades family life has altered, because of reduction in size and the giving up of traditional roles because of divorce, remarriage, and single parenthood. All of this, along with the continuing influence of the peer group, has eroded parental authority and created emotional conflicts that seem unresolvable. The generation gap is widened by lack of communication and overt concern, but haven't parents and children always had trouble dealing with each other's expectations?

Some experts regard the generation gap as a relatively new phenomenon, dating it post–World War II. If, however, we regard it as the discrepancy between the generations in roles and experience, attitudes and maturity, then surely it has always existed. Parents have always been held responsible for their children's welfare, have always had the power in the family both physically and economically. And children have always been resentful.

Along with this generational distance exists generational conflict, which experts—psychiatrists, psychologists, sociologists—interpret in different ways. While some question its presence, most regard conflict as necessary for adolescents so they can free themselves from depending on their parents, move on to responsible adulthood, and bring their unique insights to bear on the world and make it a better place in which to live.

But despite the distrust and rebellion, the furor and uproar, adolescents still turn to their parents for the answers they seek.

Four

ADOLESCENT GROWTH
AND DEVELOPMENT

Parents have always been interested in the size of their offspring. No doubt, prehistoric man stood his son against a cave wall to record his height for a variety of tribal ceremonies celebrating a boy's growth into manhood. Our current concern with height is hardly new, for ancient Greek legends tell about Procrustes, the brigand who lived along a well-traveled road and invited weary travelers to share his iron beds. If the traveler was too short for the bed, the robber simply stretched the unfortunate visitor's legs and joints until they were pulled out enough to reach the end, and if the visitor was too tall, Procrustes whacked off the legs to bring the traveler down to bed size.

Physicians today are often asked to act as a sort of scientific equivalent of that ancient bandit's custom, being called upon by parents to fit adolescents into a size frame suitable for our times. Doctors are frequently asked to retard growth when it threatens to produce an oversized girl or to increase growth when its lack seems likely to leave a boy too short. With surprising accuracy, doctors can predict growth and final adult height and can also control it with the use of hormones.

However, major questions and limitations apply to all this Procrustean medical magic today, for these practices are not really all that safe, simple, or clear. Some doctors raise serious questions about whether the emotional damage likely to be done to the youngster by his being too tall or too short warrants the use of powerful hormones to alter natural growth. Like so much else in adolescence, the physical and sexual rate of development differs vastly among individuals, which often causes unnecessary concern on the part of parents who wish the best for their children. Parents should know the whole story so that they can make an informed decision about medical intervention should there be any question of it.

RATES OF MATURATION

For the past four hundred years, children have been maturing increasingly earlier. During the last century, parents have taken for granted that their children would grow up faster, taller, and heavier than their own parents—and they've been right to assume so. It's clear from the charts of the world's leading authority on growth and development, Dr. J. M. Tanner of the University of London, that a drop in menarcheal age has been going on at a steady pace in Germany, the Scandinavian countries,

England, and the United States, with, incidentally, American women being the earliest.

Studies show that in the early 1900s the mean age of menarche was about 17.5 years, depending on what part of the globe was studied. Today, however, the most recent studies indicate that the mean age of menarche in the United States among white girls is 12.2 years and 11.5 years among black girls. In boys, too, sexual maturation has been occurring earlier in life, but the ages are not so clear-cut, simply because the evidence of male maturation cannot be as easily dated as menarche. In boys, sexual maturation is determined by evaluating such secondary characteristics as pubic hair and the gradual development of the genital organs. There are, however, some odd ways in which researchers have learned about the changing age of male maturation. Records of Johann Sebastian Bach's boys' choir in Leipzig in the eighteenth century reveal that his boys had to give up singing soprano parts because their voices changed at an average age of eighteen. But a 1959 study of London schoolboys revealed that the average age for this same voice change had dropped all the way down to 13.3 years.

The rate of growth of both height and weight and, therefore, the ultimate heights and weights of teen-agers have been steadily on the rise, especially during the past century. In the United States and Western Europe this rate of height growth—for the phenomenon involves primarily height, while weight growth has remained proportionate—has been about one inch every thirty years. In general, adults in the United States and most of the Western European countries are now some 2.5 to 3.5

inches taller than adults a hundred years ago. Today the average eighteen-year-old boy is nearly five feet nine-and-a-half inches tall. Girls average out to be five feet four-and-a-quarter inches. Dr. Tanner finds that body proportions have not altered, but that the weight gain of growing adolescents has been proportional to their size.

The reason for the trend toward bigger adolescents is far from clear. Most experts think there are a number of causes, with both genetic and environmental factors playing a role in earlier sexual maturation. Better nutrition, an improved standard of living, preventive medicine, and better health care all contribute to early maturation. But the increases now seem to be leveling off here in the United States and elsewhere; accelerated growth rates have reached a point of maximum benefit and efficiency and it is unlikely that in the future maturation will occur any earlier than it does today.

A commonly held belief suggests that menarche occurs earlier in hot climates, but this seems mistaken because Israel, for instance, has shown that menarche occurs later in Indian girls than in English or American girls; and in certain tribes in Central Africa the menarche appears between 15.5 and 16.5 years of age as compared with the United States, where it now occurs in girls under thirteen.

Dr. Tanner feels that most of the increased height and weight is simply a reflection of a more rapid maturation. He also sees nutritional factors as the probable cause of most but not all of these differences—pointing to the well-nourished Americans and West Europeans with their average menarcheal ages of roughly 12.8 to 13.2 years as contrasted with 18 years for girls in the New Guinea highlands, 17 years in parts of Central Africa, and 15.5 in the socioeconomically poor Bantu Homelands of South Africa. The well-nourished Kampala upper classes in Africa have a median menarcheal age of 13.4.

Some studies have even led to speculation that perhaps we have weeded out the weaker members of the species and are even now producing a biologically superior human being through an evolutionary process. However, we still do not know with scientific certainty what the causes for these changes are. Doctors can, however, monitor them.

For the first time in more than thirty years, the National Center for Health Statistics (NCHS) has recently brought out a major new set of pediatric growth charts based on statistics from more than twenty thousand children studied from birth to eighteen years of age. In June 1976, NCHS provided doctors with a set of fourteen computer-drawn charts that made it possible for doctors to compare the height, weight, and head circumference of their young patients with those of the rest of Americans of the same age and sex. Such comparisons improve our ability to recognize both normal and abnormal growth patterns.

The NCHS believes that teen-agers have reached the end of a long era of increasing height and weight and early biological maturation. Dr. Peter Hamill, the chairman of NCHS's task force of government and private experts, which brought out these charts, believes that this "could be the result of our having reached the limits of our genetic potential regarding growth."

Dr. Hamill admits that the cause of the end of this long increase is still not clear, but he points out that "all we can say with certainty is that whatever the factors that produced the trend to increasing size, they ceased having an effect on our rather sensitive data by 1955 or 1956 across almost all socioeconomic levels of the American population." In 1968, Dr. Tanner wrote that this worldwide trend might be leveling off in the United States, because of better nutrition, but elsewhere in the world it showed few signs of doing so.

Another interesting change that Dr. Tanner reports is that in 1900 men didn't reach their full adult height until about the age of twenty-six. But in Europe and the United States today they reach full height at eighteen or nineteen, and in France teen-agers do so even earlier. Girls in Western Europe and America, however, reach their maximal height at about sixteen or seventeen years of age.

But we must examine particular patterns of growth and maturation to help you with assessing what you see in your own teen-agers. And then we will look at what is being done today to change the patterns when it is agreed that altering nature is desirable.

PATTERNS OF GROWTH AND DEVELOPMENT

At least 25 percent of adult American men are over six feet tall, whereas before 1900 fewer than 4 percent were that tall. More than 15 percent of women are five feet seven inches tall or more, as compared to fewer than 3 percent back in 1900. All this growth happens in an odd sort of way during the teen years. While the overall size of teen-agers has obviously increased, the patterns of physical growth and development probably haven't changed since *Homo sapiens* appeared back somewhere in the mists of time, hundreds of thousands of years ago.

The patterns of adolescent growth change and the sequence of the events are generally the same in everyone. But when the changes begin, the speed with which they occur is as variable as everything else about teen-agers during this period. Growth patterns are due to the abrupt and marked changes in the levels of various hormones that until this period normally remain both low and stable. Hormones such as estrogen are "chemical messengers" produced by various endocrine glands that influence growth and metabolism and other functions of various parts of the body when carried there by the bloodstream. Estrogen levels begin to skyrocket in girls from the age of eight to eleven, and by twelve or fourteen years of age a girl's estrogen level is some twenty times its earlier one. In boys this same rise in estrogen usually occurs a year or two later, and the increase is only four times what it was earlier.

The gonadotropins (hormones produced in the pituitary gland that stimulate the reproductive glands) rise rapidly to ten times their childhood levels in sixteen-year-old girls but only to six times their earlier levels in the same age boys. In general, the development of boys seems to lag some two years behind that of girls, so that teachers often say that eighth-grade girls look like their male classmates' mothers. While these changes are going on, the pituitary gland is also involved in the production of growth hormone, which causes an increase in height but not in sexual maturity.

Certain general changes with extensive effects can be

noted. Most obvious is the rapid growth in height, weight, and muscles, and the development of sexual or biological maturity with the appearance of a female's menarche. This dynamic growth and maturation results in a particularly high bodily need for protein, calcium, and iron in addition to large amounts of calories. (The teen-agers who suffer from chronic diseases requiring dietary modifications need careful medical supervision during this period to make sure that their nutritional needs are met in spite of their special diets.) Bone changes occur too, for the skeleton grows rapidly at this time, and the gangling arms and legs so characteristic of teen-agers result. This rapid skeletal growth can lead to postural difficulties as well as athletic injuries. Careful medical supervision by a knowledgeable physician is most important. On the positive side of growing up is the fact that—perhaps because of the hormonal changes—teen-agers enjoy increased resistance to upper respiratory infections such as the common cold and sore throats.

So widely do adolescents vary in their growth patterns (in time frames, speed, and degree of development) that their chronological age is really a very poor indicator, a deceptive yardstick, of their actual developmental level. Doctors instead rely on the secondary sexual characteristics and on the "bone age" that is usually revealed by these changes taking place in the development of the hands and wrists.

In summary, we can say that the rapid increase in size and the changing shape of the body with the growth of the sexual organs occurs in both sexes but is sex-specific, different for boys and girls.

In boys a great increase in muscle size and strength takes place, a change which, as Dr. Tanner points out, prepares the boy to fulfill the primitive male primate roles (such as fighting, or foraging for food). Muscle increase is not a uniform process; the skeletal structure (the bones) and muscles take part in a growth spurt, but not at an equal or even rate. Between the ages of thirteen and fifteen and a half boys gain about forty pounds, while they add about eight inches to their height (four inches in the single year of peak height velocity). In girls, however, the growth spurt begins at about twelve years of age and is virtually completed by thirteen and a half with somewhat less growth (three-and-a-half inches, for example, in the year of peak height velocity). Following these peak years, height increases at a much slower rate, and by eighteen years of age more than 99 percent of a teen-ager's growth has usually been completed.

The order of growth follows a fairly uniform pattern, with the legs lengthening first, and then the thighs increasing in width. Then comes the increase in shoulder breadth, and finally the increase in length of the trunk. The trunk's increase is more important than the increase in length of the legs in the total height, although both together do produce the overall increase in the individual's height. The legs reach their peak growth first, followed by the trunk dimensions. The shoulders are last to reach their final breadth, so that a boy outgrows the length of his trousers a year before he outgrows his jacket. First to reach adult size are the head, the hands, and the feet, so that teen-agers—especially girls—are likely to complain about large hands and feet. However, you can reassure your teen-ager that by the time he has finally stopped growing hands and feet will be in proper proportion to the rest of the body.

The growth spurt in muscles occurs simultaneously with skeletal growth. However, while the growth of boys' muscles will reach a peak velocity much greater than that of girls', the girls reach this stage earlier—and so, from about 12.5 to 13.5 years of age, girls on the average have bigger muscles than boys. Girls achieve their maximal strength when they reach the time of menarche; boys will continue to increase in strength for a year and a half or so after they have already achieved their greatest height.

During these growth periods, fat deposition patterns also change, both in total amount and in distribution. The changes in adolescent boys have traditionally been compared to a wide rubber band being stretched out to become longer and narrower. Although boys have an increase in body fat just before puberty, recent evidence has shown that at their peak height velocity (the time of maximum acceleration of growth in height), boys actually lose fat. They regain a minimal amount after completion of their growth spurt. In girls, on the other hand, fat deposition increases at a rapid rate about a year before onset of their growth spurt, and the redistribution of fat occurs later, so that they may appear slimmer at the end of the first year of puberty. By the end of their growth spurt, however, adolescent girls have proportionately more fat than teen-age boys.

SEXUAL MATURATION

While menarche is a clear-cut dramatic incident with a precise starting time, it is only part of the total sequence of changes that mark the sexual maturation of the female. One of Dr. Tanner's important contributions in the field of human growth and development has been to classify sexual maturity into five stages that provide an accurate and convenient means of assessing the normality of the growth and sexual development of each youngster. These classifications are technical, but your doctor will use them and note what he finds on your youngster's medical chart for use in following his development.

A teen-ager's orderly passage through these stages is more important than the specific age at which they occur. The actual time of each stage is extremely variable, and the range of normality here is very wide. It is a combination of the age, height, and sexual maturity of your teen-ager that makes it possible to predict eventual height. Doctors can often predict, for example, that the fourteen-year-old boy who is five feet two inches tall and has already reached sexual maturity is going to remain shorter than average, while another lad who at this same age is shorter but who still shows no changes in his genital organs may end up a very tall adult. Yet both boys may be perfectly normal examples of the wide human diversity.

In boys, puberty usually begins with enlargement of the testes, which may occur anytime from 9.5 to 13.5 years of age. About this time the scrotum enlarges, becomes pinker, and then darkens as rugae (folds or roughnesses) appear. As scrotum, testes, and penis all enlarge, pubic hairs appear, increase, spread, darken, and curl. About a year after the beginning of the accelerated penis growth the first ejaculations of seminal fluid occur, but this event is influenced by cultural as well as biological factors.

Axillary (armpit) and facial hair growth starts about two years later than the growth of pubic hair. Body hair growth also begins about this time but may not be completed until well after puberty. The growth of facial hair follows a distinct pattern: it begins at the corners of the upper lip and spreads toward the middle; hair then appears on the upper cheeks, and following this, at the midline of the face below the lips; eventually it grows along the sides and lower borders of the chin. It is this pattern of growth that explains the kinds of mustaches and beards that teen-agers are able to grow when they first decide to stop shaving.

Johann Sebastian Bach couldn't have known it, but the change in pitch of his choirboys' voices was actually due to an enlargement of the larynx (the voicebox) and lengthening of the vocal cords. These changes result from the effect of male sex hormones (testosterone) on the laryngeal cartilage. The voice pitch first becomes variable, but the adult pitch with its change in timbre as well only appears with the final ultimate growth of the larynx to adult size late in adolescence. A breaking voice often embarrasses young boys throughout their teens. Another source of embarrassment to teen-agers (more particularly boys) is the rapid development of the axillary, genital, and anal sweat glands with the concomitant production of a characteristic odor during puberty.

Breast changes appear in both boys and girls during adolescence. (In the majority of boys this growth is mild and often imperceptible.) There may be enlargements of the areolas (the dark-colored areas surrounding the nipples). In a fifth to a quarter of boys a distinct enlargement of one or both breasts occurs, most often noticed as "a lump" by the boy during his showers. Disc-shaped and firm, this mass is deep beneath the nipple and commonly appears in midadolescence, only to disappear within a year or two. All that is really called for here is reassurance of boy and parents (discussed in detail in Chapter 15).

In five out of six girls the first sign of puberty is the appearance of the "breast bud." The beginning of that organ's growth is a small mound of breast and nipple with a slightly enlarged areola. In most girls this development is shortly followed by the appearance of straight, slightly pigmented long pubic hairs along the inner edges of the labia. In about one-sixth of adolescent girls the pubic hair may actually be the first sign of puberty. As breasts and areola enlarge with sexual maturation, these pubic hairs increase, darken, and curl, spreading out from the labia. At any time from eight to thirteen years of age, the uterus and vagina develop more fully, while the labia and clitoris enlarge. The final stage of breast development follows as the breast bud changes to a combined breast and areola contour with nipple projecting, representing essentially the adult woman's breast contour. While menarche can start at any time from ten to sixteen-and-a-half years of age, ovulation does not occur in most girls for several months following menarche, and the cycle itself is irregular more often than not during the first year or more. However, some girls *are* fertile at this time, so irregular ovulation should *not* be depended on should the youngster engage in sexual activity.

In girls it may take anywhere from one-and-a-half to six years from the time the first signs of puberty appear until sexual maturation is complete. However, these figures and times are highly variable, and only a knowledgeable doctor can tell how normally the process is unfolding. In boys, too, there is wide variation, but it takes them anywhere from two to five years to reach maturity after the onset of puberty.

In fact, perfectly normal children often alarm their parents because they don't seem to be maturing sexually. Here is a general guideline on when to seek the advice of your child's physician about suspected abnormality: puberty in girls is generally considered to be delayed when there is no breast development by the time she is thirteen, or when menarche has not occurred within four years after breast development. In boys, puberty is regarded as delayed when there is no testicle enlargement by the age of thirteen and a half. But it takes a trained doctor to interpret the many variations properly.

MODERN MEDICAL CONTROL

Many youngsters suffer a variety of medical disorders that affect growth—conditions such as those that produced Josef Winkelmaier, the Austrian who died in 1887 at the age of twenty-two at the height of eight feet nine inches; or Charles Stratton, the circus midget, whom P. T. Barnum made famous as General Tom Thumb. Tumors and other disorders of the pituitary gland can cause the gland to be either over- or underactive. An overactive gland, or specifically overproduction of human growth hormone (HGH), leads to the giantism of which Winkelmaier was a prime example. An underactive gland causes a lack of HGH and produces a dwarf such as Tom Thumb. Other disorders (such as certain brain tumors, skull fractures, or infections) can also affect the pituitary gland and produce growth disturbances. Thyroid gland conditions that reduce hormone production can also interfere with growth. Obviously these conditions or any other disorders or diseases call for medical investigation, although actually these are rather rare conditions and their treatment has been carefully defined.

An issue of a highly regarded medical magazine, *Medical World News* of February 23, 1976, estimated that hundreds of thousands of teen-agers along with their parents are today seeking medical help to make the short youngster taller and keep the tall from becoming excessively so. Pressed by anxious and concerned parents (it's often more the parents' problem than the youngsters') and by worried adolescents, doctors occasionally send one of these youngsters to a pediatric endocrinologist (a specialist in hormonal problems of the young). Yet probably only a minority of those referred for a suspected endocrine disorder actually have such a problem. In fact, actual endocrine disease accounts for only a small percentage of all youngsters with growth disturbances.

If an adolescent's growth has been less than two inches

in a given year, there is cause for concern, particularly if the previous annual growth was more than that. Doctors should compare the heights of the family members and carefully examine the youngster using blood and urine tests and even X-rays, usually of the wrists. The most common causes of shortness are genetic (inherited) and those due to a delayed growth pattern. When the cause is genetic, both parents, one or more siblings, and several grandparents will also be short.

If the youngster is troubled by his height, he should be treated only with psychological counseling. Some physicians, however, feel that in some cases of delayed growth, psychological problems may warrant the use of male sex hormones. Both teen-ager and parents must be warned of the possible loss of one to two inches from the eventual adult height if hormones are used. Hormones speed up development of the growth centers at the ends of the long bones, thereby accelerating the end of height growth, which might last longer without hormones.

One rare cause of short stature has probably gotten more publicity than any other: the lack of HGH, or what is called pituitary dwarfism. Its symptoms are shortness and delayed puberty with smaller-than-average genitals and, in some boys, undescended testicles. Three times as many boys as girls lack HGH. Youngsters suffering pituitary dwarfism usually look much younger than they are and tend to be overweight for their height. Half may lack only HGH, while the other half may lack other pituitary hormones as well. The causes of pituitary dwarfism are various, and not all of them are yet understood.

Tests for HGH deficiency include bone age and skull X-rays and checking HGH levels in the blood. The deficiency is treated by injections of HGH, but its supply is limited in the United States (HGH is extracted from human pituitary glands at autopsies), and so its use is restricted to those whose need is greatest.

Of course, the big problem here is how to decide what is "too short" and "too tall." A look at the newspapers, history books, and sports and fashion pages shows how short men or tall women succeed in an unending variety of occupations and careers. Height is often a distinguishing factor in career choice (consider racing jockeys and fashion models). It's a difficult question, and parents might well examine their own feelings carefully before imposing a standard on their children. As one mother of a tall daughter admitted, she had been miserable as a five-foot-ten-inch young girl thirty years ago. She failed to realize that today all teen-agers are taller, and since roughly one-quarter of all men are now six feet or more, a five-foot-ten-inch girl such as her daughter was at no disadvantage other than the mother's emotional reaction and the girl's resulting confusion.

Doctors carry out a careful and thorough physical and laboratory examination when there is real cause for concern. By using present height, bone age X-rays, and the teen-ager's present level of sexual maturation, doctors can make a fairly accurate projection of what the adolescent's height will be when he becomes an adult, but they often have to watch the youngster carefully for some years before any definitive prediction can be made.

For girls who are considered to be excessively tall, say

with a predicted adult height of five feet eleven inches, treatment has heretofore been high doses of various female sex hormones (estrogens). In one study, eighty-seven youngsters were given a one-year program, and all but five reached a final height that was 1.4 to 2.4 inches less than their predicted adult heights. The psychological benefit was even greater. However, treatment should be started as soon before the onset of puberty as can be determined, although it may be (and often is) started a year or two later. This is to avoid the psychological embarrassment of precocious puberty and imbalance in the menstrual cycle. Menstrual disturbances, the most common side effects of estrogen therapy, can be corrected by adding another hormone to the first. The less common side effects of increased pigmentation of the areolas and obesity will disappear upon cessation of therapy, of which both teen-ager and parents should be made aware before treatment begins. With hormone treatments the youngster is likely to pass through puberty to sexual maturation much more quickly.

Surely the key question must be what dangers these measures carry with them. To interfere with an individual's normal growth and development is a radical step. Many doctors feel strongly that psychological consultation is a much wiser approach to concern over height than is interfering with natural growth processes. In any case, the matter should be carefully thought out and fully discussed with the youngster's doctor.

Five

ADOLESCENTS AND SEX

THE sexual behavior of today's teen-agers is one of the most distressing problems physicians and parents face and it is troublesome to the youngsters themselves as well. The problem is disturbing because its roots lie buried in our complex background of religion and culture, social attitudes, values, and beliefs. The ultimate resolution will surely be difficult, painful, and long in coming, and it may well necessitate major changes in our entire social structure. Compounding and confusing the picture are the biological, physical, mental health, and genetic problems inherent in the current teen-age difficulties with venereal disease, contraception, pregnancy, abortion, and adoption. These, in turn, are aggravated by the psychological problems involved in the generational clash and the adolescent's need to carry out his developmental tasks.

What not too long ago was denigratingly termed "shacking up" has now acquired the respectability of widespread social practice and acceptance. Nevertheless, it may still present major emotional and personal problems to many American teen-agers' parents, most of whom are in their forties or older, and the majority of whom regard as morally wrong the widespread current practice of cohabitation. It is significant that society does not yet have any widely accepted term for this setup, or for the young men and women involved in such relationships.

Living together is not in fact a real innovation. It's been around since marriage was incorporated into human society. Only today has living together become an open lifestyle. Standards are becoming confused, and nobody can say what's right. Take, for example, the middle-aged couple who were originally shocked when they discovered that their first son was living with a young woman. It no longer upset them when son number two moved in with a girl, but they objected when son number three announced he was going to marry a girl they felt unsuitable. They urged him to try living with her instead, only to find the boy shocked at the idea. Only marriage seemed right and proper to him for their relationship!

At the bottom of this confusion is simply the underlying issue of sexual relations between unmarried couples, new only in the openness and perhaps the extent of the current practice. Parents today are not so much concerned about teen-age sex itself as about early and promiscuous relations. Often early sex endangers the adolescent's emotional and physical health. The lack of contraception, the problems created by the current epidemic of venereal disease, and the multitude of teen-age pregnancies are just some of the complications resulting from early sexual relations. All these issues cast their shadow across the susceptible and often naïve young people who thrust themselves forward into areas whose dangers they either cannot imagine or choose to ignore.

That we are now in the midst of a sexual upheaval is clear—although the smoke and fury that always accompany such major changes tend to obscure the reality of what is actually going on. No one really knows where we are, much less where we are going. The experts argue and disagree, and statistics vary widely even on such a simple question as how much more common premarital sex is today.

Amidst such confusion, let us look at the facts and figures available in the areas of sexual behavior, contraception, pregnancy, abortion, adoption, and venereal disease in order to secure some basis for determining parental and adolescent responsibility. Such information may help protect you and your teen-ager. We will try to provide specific information on specific questions. Let's begin at the root of it all.

TEEN-AGE SEX: ROLE AND REALITY

Teen-agers undeniably experience sexual drives, but there is in fact good reason to question whether adolescent sexual activity has changed all that much in the last fifty years. Perhaps it has always been much the same, except for the alterations produced by present-day early maturation and menarche, which may be why there are so many more unwanted teen-age pregnancies than ever before.

Some observers of adolescent behavior feel that the real sexual revolution may well be more attitudinal than behavioral. They say that teen-agers talk more openly about sex, that they no longer regard sex as sinful, that most no longer adhere to the "double standard" that condemns only female premarital sex. However, studies by Drs. R. C. Sorenson, John F. Kantner, and Melvin Zelnick in 1976 showed a definite increase in adolescent female premarital sexual activity between the ages of fifteen and nineteen. But researchers and many pediatricians observe controlled sex among teen-agers—that is to say, sexual intercourse with a limited number of partners, if not just with one.

Parents these days are disturbed by the flood of figures on the percentages of youngsters who indulge in sex, but figures may be more easily attainable now than in the past. The figures do vary considerably from authority to authority. Many experts assert that 25 percent of teen-age girls have had sex, while others say it is 30 to 40 percent. The figures for boys are commonly regarded as being roughly double those for girls. But regardless of the sexual revolution and the talk of sexual equality, the promiscuous teen-age girl is still looked down on.

Some of the most highly regarded studies in the area of teen-age sexuality were conducted by Drs. Melvin Zelnik and John F. Kantner, sociologists at Johns Hopkins. They found that 28 percent of the group of unmarried girls aged fifteen to nineteen that they studied had had sex, although half of them had had none in the month previous to the study. Among the half who had had sex recently, nine out of ten had had it with one particular boy. Their most recent report (1978) finds that among the fifteen- to nineteen-year-old girls studied in 1971, three out of ten had had sex, whereas by 1976 the rate had risen to four out of ten, with a percentage increase greater among whites (41 percent) than among blacks (19 percent). Dr. Daniel T. Gianturco, a Duke University professor of psychiatry, finds that despite the attitudinal changes in adolescents today, teen-agers on the whole turn down casual and indiscriminate sex, preferring to use sex as part of a close and lasting relationship.

It is obviously difficult to determine the causes of the increase. Peer pressure as well as social attitudes are factors. The advent of the pill and of antibiotics has freed males and females from the old twin fears of conception and infection. With society's new permissive attitude, teen-agers need no longer fear detection. At times it seems as though they proudly flaunt their sexual activity as another weapon in the age-old generational conflict.

What concerns mental health experts, as well as physicians interested in the physical well-being of their patients, is that young people who start sexual activity at a very young age usually suffer definite damage to their capacity for developing psychological intimacy in the future. On the other hand, teen-agers who become well acquainted with each other before they have sex are much more likely to develop good and long-lasting relationships.

How teen-agers deal with the problem of their burgeoning sexuality depends on a host of factors—peer pressure, the information and ideas about sex that come from the news media, and other sources. A 1975 Wayne State University report revealed the origins of the sexual knowledge of 1,200 Detroit teen-agers (88 percent of them female) who came from the upper high school grades and from all socioeconomic levels. Their information regarding sex came first from friends; second, from the mass media; third, from parents; fourth, from teachers and school counselors. Physicians ran a poor fifth (only 16 percent asked doctors for sexual information). In short, young people present a classic example of the halt leading the blind—that explains why youngsters are so naïve and ignorant about sex.

Tragically, vital decisions about sexual behavior—decisions and actions likely to affect their entire lives in many ways—are made today by adolescents during the most confused and tumultuous period of their lives, and at a time when society offers minimal guidelines as compared with the past. Ideally, these young people would have had an early sexual education starting in the home during the preschool years. If this were followed by good sex education in the schools, an open line of communication would remain throughout the teen years. Youngsters who come from a home in which there has always been free discussion of anything the child wished to ask about should have minimal problems in the area of sexuality.

The chief problem stems from poor sex education at all levels, at home and in the school. Sex education should start in the preteen years—say at the age of ten or eleven (grades five and six)—and it must be reinforced regularly and strongly with necessary changes as children reach the age of twelve or fourteen (grades seven to nine) and beyond.

Youngsters are confused by the wide variety of ideas

about sexuality that flood in through the various media. The different news presented makes it difficult for them to know exactly what the right sexual standards are. Open and informed family and school discussions of sexual problems and concepts are recommended. Providing proper reading materials and holding open discussions to help in forming these young people's concepts is especially valuable.

It's also valuable to have a doctor who is adept at dealing with teen-agers and can handle questions about sexuality. At this stage of life the adolescent's fight for independence and hostility toward parental authority make it difficult to involve the youngster with a physician—for all doctors may be viewed, consciously or unconsciously, as a parent surrogate. But a sensitive, competent doctor can provide youngsters with the appropriate reading materials or answer any questions they may have.

Dr. Harry Gershman, dean of the American Institute for Psychoanalysis in New York and a leading analyst, is deeply concerned with our so-called sexual revolution. His point is clear: "I have the feeling that too often sex has become as plastic as most other things in our society. Sex used to be the last bastion of individuality and self-hood. . . . Now it is too often cast into mass production molds." He worries lest people be dehumanized into "well-functioning sex machines that do not really connect with inner selves from which spring warmth, tenderness, caring communication, affection, and love."

Dr. Gershman's view is one that all of us might use as the basis for real growth and change today: "When freed from centuries of our cultural-religious repression—because it was considered animalistic, sinful, dirty, and taboo—sexuality will come more truly into its rightful place as a human experience that affords participants greater pleasure, mutuality, affection, and relatedness than any other experience." This thinking might well be used as the basis for open family discussions to help the teen-agers explore healthy new attitudes about sexuality, while simultaneously causing them to pause before accepting the views of peers and the media, to which they tend to respond so readily and uncritically.

PREGNANCY

Pregnancy among teen-age girls today has reached epidemic proportions, almost a million in 1975, more than two million now. Pregnancy—often followed by abortion or putting the unwanted baby up for adoption—and the exploding rate of venereal disease cause many psychological and physical problems. The whole question of teen-age sexuality is fraught with health-care problems.

Studies from the National Institutes of Health (NIH) reveal that in 1975 more than half a million teen-agers gave birth; some thirty thousand young women got legal abortions, and no one knows how many aborted illegally. Two hundred and twenty-four thousand of these births were to unmarried teen-agers, and over twelve thousand were to girls under the age of fifteen. Between 1960 and 1973 the number of children born to girls under the age of sixteen jumped 80 percent and by 25 percent among the sixteen- and seventeen-year-olds. In 1977, 600,000 teen-agers gave birth.

Dr. Thomas F. McDonald of San Diego's Imperial County Community Health Center and Drs. Zelnik and Kantner of Johns Hopkins find that very few of these teen-agers want to get pregnant. An unwanted pregnancy will certainly play havoc with an adolescent's already confused world. Pregnancy also causes the immature and vacillating teen-age mother a host of further problems: Should she have the baby and give it up for adoption, or should she have an abortion? Should she try for a forced marriage? What should she do about her schooling, which will probably be interrupted because of local school regulations? She must also deal with the anger and resentment of her family and face possible rejection by family and boyfriend. The young pregnant teen-ager is likely to be socially isolated. As one girl complained, "I was treated like an outcast—everybody was against me!"

To make matters worse, pregnancy that takes place before the end of adolescence is susceptible to complications that can be dangerous to young mothers and their babies. The earlier the pregnancy, the greater the danger. The physical and psychological health of the teen-ager may suffer: a high incidence of toxemia, a life-threatening bacterial blood infection, in early adolescence, is not unusual. Cesarean section may be necessary; there may be prolonged labor and premature birth. The infant is often underdeveloped and may suffer more birth defects than the children of adults. After all, the optimal time for having children is between the ages of twenty and twenty-nine, with the best period between twenty and twenty-four. Girls should not have children before they are nineteen years old.

Pregnancy in adolescence has a different emotional impact at different ages. Because of their limited rationality and ability for abstract thought as well as their incomplete personality development, most girls ages eleven to thirteen lack understanding of both contraceptive measures and the reality and consequences of pregnancy. They may dissociate themselves from blame and refuse to accept the responsibilities of being pregnant. They can be reluctant to visit a doctor or clinic and to follow sound principles of prenatal care.

During the midadolescent years—from fourteen through sixteen—the girls are further along in their intellectual development. Although aware of contraceptive measures, they may well refuse to use them in order to defy parents or to test their womanhood. When these girls become pregnant they are ambivalent, feeling both guilt and pride. They blame parents or boyfriend. They often feel that motherhood proves their maturity and means independence, yet many also become depressed at the prospect of such responsibility. As rebellion and antagonism increase, the parent–child conflict grows, and this antagonism spreads to their dealings with doctor, nurse, and social worker.

In later adolescence a girl's intellectual powers become fully established. These more mature teen-agers usually accept the responsibility when they become pregnant and blame no one but themselves. Many may hope for marriage, but most older girls opt for abortion.

Sex is one of the manifestations of adolescent behavior—and since teen-age girls are sexually active and potentially fertile at younger ages than ever before, more pregnancies result. Whether this is due to the openness in our society concerning sexuality or whether we are too sexually preoccupied is still an open question. But we should view the pregnant adolescent as someone who may be having problems with her own psychological development that are more pervasive and more general than the question of sexuality—she may be suffering from conflicts involving dependency, identity, self-esteem, and the group values and standards in her particular community.

If the professionals involved with the pregnant teen-ager don't recommend solutions such as contraception, pregnancy will become a repeated occurrence in a revolving-door sort of situation. Physicians must understand what the issues are for teen-agers and offer their support to be sure that the experience fosters healthy growth and development. The teen-ager will herself lead the doctor to the solution if she feels she can trust him. Often the pregnancy itself is a cry for help, meant to attract attention to her underlying psychological problems. With understanding, families and doctors together can help the pregnant young woman understand her own problems and make the solution permanent.

In an extensive 1971 nationwide survey of the sexual contraceptive and pregnancy experiences of fifteen- to nineteen-year-old girls, Drs. Zelnik and Kantner found that more than half the unmarried teen-agers in the United States who had sex did not use any contraception during their last sexual encounter. Fewer than one out of five always used contraception. However, by 1976 this situation had improved, so that more than one out of four were always using contraception, but the percentage who are using contraceptives varies among racial groups. It is mostly because teen-agers engage only in sporadic and unanticipated sex that they practice contraception erratically and unreliably. It is rare that pregnancy results from one-night stands, however. Usually it is a consequence of an ongoing relationship in which the naïve teen-agers do not take regular or adequate precaution. Actually it is the "promiscuous" teen-agers—those who have sex frequently—who do use contraceptive techniques routinely and effectively.

THE DILEMMA OF
ABORTION OR ADOPTION

But how is teen-age pregnancy resolved? Abortion or giving the infant up for adoption have been the answers of the past. Almost as many teen-agers had abortions in 1975 as had babies. However, both abortion and adoption entail grief and loss. Whether the pregnancy is aborted or the infant is given away for adoption, the psychological reaction is in response to separation; in short, there is bereavement.

Abortion or adoption must be a decision based on reality. Who is to care for and pay for the new child? If the father cannot support the new family—and how many teen-age boys can?—the responsibility devolves on the young mother's parents or perhaps on both mother's and father's parents. The girl isn't likely to go back to school, but neither will she have time for a job. The baby's welfare must be considered, as well as the mother's.

Teen-agers often cannot understand what it means to be a parent to a child: the limitations and sacrifices of parenthood will prevent an adolescent from enjoying ordinary pursuits. This limitation of freedom must be recognized by the pregnant young woman so that she can decide whether to carry through the pregnancy or to abort. Professional advice from a psychiatrist, social worker, or adolescent physician may be needed, since the generational conflict and the natural rebelliousness of the adolescent make it difficult for parents to communicate with their daughters at such a time.

In teen-age abortions religious scruples sometimes produce extra problems above and beyond those associated with bereavement. Sometimes the psychological loss is paramount. Experts find that a woman of any age who has chosen abortion often unconsciously searches for the lost child. Such a longing may lead to recurrent pregnancies in a psychological attempt to replace the infant. Thus the very loss of a baby may lead to continued sexual activity—and more pregnancies, unless the young woman undertakes contraception.

It would seem that the earlier the termination of pregnancy is carried out for a teen-ager, the easier is the loss. A first trimester abortion is easier than an adoption. The further a woman goes with her pregnancy, the harder it is for her to give up the child. In fact, most adolescents who have their babies and then give them up for adoption suffer a loss that they never really overcome.

The teen-age girl who goes through an abortion needs skilled professional counseling. And for the pregnant teen-ager, a sensitive physician or obstetrician who knows adolescents well is certainly needed—someone the teen-ager can relate to, trust, and feel comfortable with. Unwanted pregnancy is so painful for many families that professional help might well be sought also by the parents to ease their own anguish.

Teen-agers eighteen or nineteen years old may choose deliberately to become pregnant. They may be mature enough to handle the demands of childbearing.

Only recently has the boy—the teen-age father—been considered in teen-age pregnancies. Most young fathers are frightened, confused, and guilt-laden, almost incapable of believing that pregnancy is the result of their sexual activity. But many young fathers want to be consulted in the fates of their children, and they too will need professional guidance. The boys who prefer not to have anything to do with their pregnant girlfriends need counseling as well. Fathers should bear some of the responsibility and should not be left out of the decision-making process.

TEEN-AGE CONTRACEPTIVE TECHNIQUES

Contraception has always been primarily the girl's problem, especially since condoms have now been largely replaced as a means of contraception. The whole question of contraception has suddenly taken on new meaning, as some of the seemingly ideal solutions (the birth-control pill for one) have in practice proven to have serious drawbacks and even dangers. Clearly there is not yet a perfect means of contraception for providing efficacy and safety with comfort and convenience.

The best approach for parents to take toward sex and contraception is to bring the premenarcheal girl to a physician (either an adolescent physician or a gynecologist or obstetrician) who can explain the reproductive system to the youngster, dispel the myths about menarche and the menstrual cycle, and explain as well the availability, kinds, advantages, and disadvantages of current contraceptive measures. Such doctors can also at this time discuss the youngster's future sexual activity and the problems of pregnancy, along with a rational approach to sexuality and the scientific reasons for waiting until she is emotionally mature enough for sexual activity. Doctors can provide her with appropriate booklets on contraception and venereal disease and answer questions. Besides giving her an open line of communication if she needs advice or help at any time, a visit to a doctor also gives a young woman the opportunity to plan rationally for her sexual life with the help of a knowledgeable adult interested in her welfare.

Contraception today is an area of much research, and many of the current concerns about the pill and intra-uterine devices (IUDs) will surely be clarified as new techniques are introduced in the future. Many physicians and other parents don't want their daughters to use the pill because of its dangers, such as hypertension (high blood pressure), which is more common after one year of use, and blood clots in deep veins (or, rarely, strokes), the risk of which is lessened by low-dose estrogen. The pill can also inhibit growth if used regularly before the youngster has reached full adult growth, say at the age of twelve or fourteen. The pill should only be taken by teen-agers under medical supervision. Experts advise that teen-agers should have their blood pressure checked regularly once a month for four or five months after starting on the pill and then once a year thereafter. They should also have tests of blood components. Nervousness, irritability, and fatigue have been observed by some doctors in a significant number of teen-agers on the pill.

Some physicians still regard the condom and a spermicidal jelly as the best choice for young couples having occasional intercourse. While condoms and jellies, foams, or creams used separately are each about 80 percent effective, their combined use gives about 99 percent contraceptive effectiveness. However, the creams must be inserted into the vagina thirty minutes before anticipated sexual intercourse and orgasm. This is not always feasible for many impulsive teen-agers.

The diaphragm, a dome-shaped cup of rubber stretched over a flexible ring, must be filled with spermicidal jelly and inserted into the vagina. It must be fitted snugly over the uterine cervix about one hour or more before use. It must not be removed until six to eight hours later. Both insertion and removal require practice and skill. The effectiveness of a diaphragm and spermicidal jelly is about 95 percent, and they are safer than either the pill or an IUD.

The IUD (intrauterine device) is a soft plastic (or plastic and copper) coil that must be inserted into the uterus at the end of a menstrual period by a physician. Its effectiveness is about 97 percent, but about 12 percent of the IUDs inserted are expelled spontaneously (especially in women who have never given birth) and 4 percent cause local irritation or backaches. While many IUDs have been left in place for a year or more, their usage requires frequent visits to a gynecologist. Finally, and most importantly, there is a three- to sevenfold increase in the risk of acute salpingitis (Fallopian tube inflammation and/or infection) and pelvic abscess due to the use of an IUD. Another comparison shows the magnitude of the problem: pelvic inflammatory disease (known as PID) occurs in 13 out of 100,000 pill users and in 66 out of 100,000 IUD users. Because of these adverse reactions, the Food and Drug Administration requires that women be provided with a brochure on the potential risks before having an IUD inserted. Diaphragms are most effective when properly and conscientiously used by teen-agers who have sex only infrequently. Oral contraceptives and intrauterine devices are the most commonly used means of preventing pregnancy in adolescent girls. The risks from oral contraceptives are less than the risks of pregnancy during adolescence. With carefully instructed, faithful compliance in the taking of the pill, oral contraceptives are the most effective method of preventing conception, especially for girls who have sexual intercourse regularly (weekly or every two weeks).

VENEREAL DISEASES

The word *venereal* comes from *Venus*, the Roman goddess of love, but the diseases that bear her name can hardly be considered gifts of love. Venereal diseases (VD) are "sexually transmitted diseases," of which there are four-teen types. They have plagued humanity for a long time—gonorrhea was known to the Chinese over five thousand years ago. Today the only infectious disease more common than VD is the common cold. More than twice as many cases of VD are reported to the U.S. Public Health Service's Center for Disease Control (CDC) as all other reportable communicable diseases combined. In 1976, 1977, and 1978 one million cases of gonorrhea and eighty thousand cases of syphilis were reported. Experts estimate that 2 to 8 million more cases of gonorrhea went unre-ported. There are about eight hundred thousand cases of nongonococcal urethritis (NGU) per year. Twenty-five percent of the VD cases, now more properly called STD (sexually transmissible diseases) occurred in the fifteen- to nineteen-year-old group. The majority of gonorrhea cases were in the fifteen to twenty-nine age group.

Gonorrhea, the most prevalent of the sexually transmit-ted diseases, is caused by a bacterial organism called *Neisseria gonorrhoeae*, which can be found in the genital tract, oropharynx (mouth and gullet), and anal canal. Descriptions of this disease can be found in the earliest histories of humankind. Galen named it for "flow of seed" in A.D. 100. Infection is almost always the result of contact with an infected area. After an incubation period of two to ten days, a male who has contracted the gonorrhea organism genitally will develop symptoms 95 percent of the time. Symptoms are painful, burning, difficult urina-tion and a purulent (pus-containing) discharge from the urethra (penis opening). Diagnosis can be confirmed with 99 percent accuracy by an examination of a urethral smear under a microscope, followed by a culture of that smear. In women, symptoms may be nonspecific, such as urinary frequency, difficulty of urinating, or vaginal discharge, or they may be altogether absent, as happens in the majority of female cases. In addition, smears of the female urethra are of limited value, since about 40 percent of results are falsely negative. A culture from the cervix (neck of the uterus) is more diagnostic than one from the urethra, but anal culture in women with genital gonorrhea is positive in 30 to 50 percent of the cases, presumably because of the close proximity or contiguity of these structures. Treatment for both sexes is injected penicillin or oral ampicillin, or, for penicillin-allergic patients, spectinomycin.

Nongonococcal urethritis is a sexually transmissible disease that is more prevalent than gonorrhea in England, though not in the United States. It is caused by one of two known organisms in the majority of cases. (*Chlamydia trachomatis* is about half of all cases and *Ureaplasma urealyticum* in a quarter of all cases and by no known organism in another quarter of all cases). Its incubation period is longer, between one and three weeks, and the disease is less severe than gonorrhea insofar as discharge is less profuse (but more mucoid and less pus-containing). The difficulty with urination is also less severe. Diagnosis must be confirmed by smear and culture in men; women generally do not contract the disease. Treatment is with oral tetracycline or erythrocin for seven to ten days (or up to three weeks, according to some urologists).

A sexually transmissible disease caused by the spirochete *Treponema pallidum*, syphilis is acquired 95 percent of the time by sexual exposure. The remaining cases may be transmitted by moist kisses (not dry pecks), by accidental inoculation in the laboratory by handling treponemas, by blood transfusion (a rare source nowadays), or prenatally (mother to fetus). It is diagnosed by the appearance of a primary lesion, called a chancre, of the genital area, most commonly the labia of females or the corona (rim of the end of the penis) of males. But the chancre may also appear on lips, face, tongue, fingers, breasts, or abdomen. The chancre is initially a pimple or blister that evolves into a hard, nontender ulcer with raised, smooth, and sharply defined edges. It may have a scanty yellowish discharge, and it is painless. That's why it may go undiscovered, especially in the female genitals, which are not usually thoroughly inspected. While the venereal disease research laboratory (VDRL) test is useful in screening for this disease its disadvantage is that it may take one or two weeks after appearance of the chancre for the VDRL to become positive. True confirmation of the existence of syphilis may be made only by finding spirochetes on darkfield examination, using a standard microscope under low-intensity light. However, a new test is available for quick confirmation; it's called the rapid plasma reagin card (RPRC) test and is becoming available throughout the country. Although the ulcer or chancre of primary syphilis will heal in one or two weeks, the untreated patient may go on to develop secondary or latent stages, the latter of which may be severely crippling or fatal. Treatment of primary syphilis must be accomplished with intramuscular injections of long-acting benzathine penicillin, or of short-acting penicillin several times, or, for patients sensitive to penicillin, with oral tetracycline, erythromycin, or doxycycline for twelve days.

Other sexually transmissible diseases are caused by a host of disease agents, such as the bacterium *Hemophilus vaginalis*, the parasite Trichomonas, and numerous viruses. The prevalence and importance of virus-caused STD has increased greatly during the past decade. Genital warts (condylomata acuminata) are skin and mucous membrane infections due to a virus. They occur most commonly as a result of sexual contact and appear after an incubation period of one to three (up to eight) months. They are dense clusters of outgrowing tissue around the anus, on the genitals, and even in the urethra of males and upper vagina or cervix of females. The warts are painful and the preferred mode of treatment, a chemical marketed under the brand name Podophyllin applied for six hours or more, may also be painful. Some of the most severe cases may require surgical removal.

The herpes simplex virus, formerly the cause only of annoying "cold sores" or "fever blisters" at the angles of the mouth, has become a major nuisance among STDs, especially in girls and women. It is properly known as herpesvirus, types 1 and 2. Type 1 is the cause of sores on the gums, lesions in and around the mouth, infection of the brain, and in 5 to 10 percent of the cases, of genital herpes. Type 2 herpesvirus is associated with lesions of the genitals or skin sites below the waist, particularly thighs and buttocks. Symptoms occur when one or more tiny blisters ulcerate over thirty-six to forty-eight hours and produce redness, edema (swelling), and discomfort or pain. The majority of cases in adults are subclinical—that is, either with rapid evolution and disappearance of lesions or without pain. Recurrence is common during the first year. Treatment is limited to oral pain relievers and topical soothing agents for skin and mucous lesions. For herpesvirus of the cornea and for that of a newborn infant, specific topicals are available. For encephalitis caused by herpesvirus, a potent oral agent with the brand name Arabinoside A (ARA-A) is used. At the extreme of treatment modalities, when genital herpes is discovered or suspected in a pregnant woman at or near term, prevention of very serious or fatal disease of the infant requires cesarean section. Probably the best preventive measure for genital herpesvirus infection is avoidance of promiscuous sexual behavior. However, this must not be misconstrued, since not all genital herpesvirus type 2 is contracted by sexual means.

Teen-agers are strangely naïve about VD; perhaps a belief in the magic powers of drugs and antibiotics enables them to ignore both the dangers of promiscuous sex and the precautions against disease. Checkups as soon as the symptoms of sores or discharges appear are imperative. VD may not produce symptoms, so an infected person can transmit the disease without knowing it. In gonorrhea, for example, 75 percent of women infected have no symptoms; some experts say that 10 to 40 percent of males don't either. Patients often show up in doctors' offices with late symptoms of syphilis. The symptoms can vary, but they should not be ignored. Syphilis can be fatal.

Open lines of communication between teen-agers and parents can allow free discussion of these problems, and a physician can recommend appropriate reading material giving the latest information. Schools are also making information on VD increasingly available, so that teen-agers will be aware of the dangers. Teen-agers tend to refuse to believe much of what is told them, and fear of infection seems to have no deterrent effect. New approaches are obviously needed. Even though Denmark has developed its sex education programs to high degree, it has not been able to reduce the rate of gonorrhea among its young people. Also distressing is the fact that new forms of gonorrhea are resistant to penicillin and may pose serious threats to the control of this disease in the future.

A useful source of information is the National Institute of Allergy and Infectious Diseases (Bethesda, Md. 20014) material on sexually transmitted diseases. Writing this institute, a branch of the National Institutes of Health, will bring you the latest authoritative information on whichever of the many forms of VD are currently raging. What we must all hope for are quick, simple blood tests for detecting VD and better methods of control and prevention.

Six

ALCOHOL, MARIJUANA, AND CIGARETTES: THE TRIPLE THREAT

ALCOHOL is the number-one drug problem among teen-agers today. Marijuana runs a close second.

A survey commissioned by the New York City affiliate of the National Council on Alcoholism found that only 2 teen-agers out of 108 in an affluent metropolitan New York high school did not drink. Another study in a Long Island high school found that 90 percent of 300 students drank.

The problem is rapidly growing, and it is national in scope. The National Institute of Alcohol Abuse and Alcoholism (NIAAA) in the last two months of 1976 reviewed 120 surveys of junior and senior high school drinking practices and found that 70 percent (7 percent more boys than girls)—almost 17 million of today's in-school teen-agers—drink.

The National Institute on Drug Abuse (NIDA) reports that in 1976 the number of teen-agers who had ever used marijuana ranged from 6 percent among the twelve and thirteen year olds to a high of 53 percent among the eighteen to twenty-five year olds. The percentage of teen-agers using "hard drugs" (such as heroin or amphetamines) is small in comparison.

Parents need to understand this indulgence, to have some way of predicting who is likely to become a drug abuser, so that they can take action to prevent it or to deal more effectively with teen-agers when it does happen.

Alcohol and drugs are nearly as old as humankind. The ancient witch doctors and medicine men turned to familiar plants—herbs, berries, leaves and flowers—to provide relief from pain. The wild grape is a primitive plant—fossil leaves indicate it was present at least 75 million years ago. It was probably part of human culture at least twelve thousand years ago. Alcoholic beverages were probably discovered much earlier, when human beings first came down out of the trees—for all they had to do was leave their collected fruits and berries exposed to the then-existing climatic conditions and a crude wine would soon have developed. Experts believe that humans moved from this accidental discovery of alcoholic drinks to its deliberate production and use. The alcoholic problem is a long-existing American one, for beer came over on the *Mayflower* with the Pilgrims. The early pioneers and settlers were hard-drinking, and during the Revolutionary War the surgeon-general, Dr. Benjamin Rush, termed the abuse of alcohol a "disease" and an "addiction." Even then it was a serious national problem.

Opium has probably been known and used as a painkiller since the Stone Age. An early Sumerian clay tablet dating from at least five thousand years ago refers to it. The use of marijuana was recorded in Chinese medical texts of about that same period. The early Egyptians and Hindus mixed it with wine to relieve surgical pain.

The introduction of hypodermic injections of morphine (an opium derivative) in 1853 by a Dr. Alexander Wood for the local relief of neuralgic pain heralded our modern addiction problems. Dr. Wood's wife is said to have been the first to fall prey to morphine addiction by injection. Physicians injected opiates and morphine so freely into our Civil War wounded that narcotic addiction was known as "the soldier's disease." Opium and morphine were used generously in patent medicines. With no government restrictions, these medicines were available in the general store as well as the pharmacy. Addiction was widespread throughout the population.

Ironically, a number of our most addictive drugs have been introduced as cures for other addictions. In 1884 Sigmund Freud wrote that cocaine could be used to cure morphine addiction, and in 1898 Germany's Bayer Company introduced heroin as an effective new painkiller that was both safe and nonaddictive, unlike morphine, from which it was derived. Today heroin is probably our deadliest addictive drug, and it has been estimated that 75 percent of the drug addicts on the East Coast use it. Heroin addiction was primarily a disease of the prisons and the city ghettos until it was taken over by our young people during the social upheavals of the 1960s, when it spread to the "Golden Ghettos," the affluent suburbs of the middle and upper class.

In an interview with alcohol- and drug-using teen-agers, Dr. Leroy C. Gould and colleagues at the Yale University

School of Medicine found the following: Three-quarters of the students studied had used alcohol, over half had tried marijuana, and one-third hashish; some 18 percent had used barbiturates; 12 percent, LSD; 10 percent, mescaline; 6 percent, cocaine; and 2 percent, heroin. Such polydrug abuse (multiple drugs used either successively or simultaneously) should be a matter of great concern. Dr. Gould's figures indicate the frequency of drug use. Multiple drug use in this study was widespread, with 58 percent of the students reporting having used more than one drug and 44 percent having used three or more. And 43 percent were still using multiple drugs at the time the team surveyed them.

THE DANGERS OF DRUGS

Drugs have been used in all societies, but Americans reacted emotionally to the sudden and disturbing proliferation of drug use in the 1960s when the "drug scene" spread to the middle- and upper-class teen-agers. Looking rationally at the situation, we must recognize that ours has become a pill-popping society, a culture whose drug-taking probably exceeds that of any other in history. Witness, for example, the amounts of alcohol, cigarettes, and coffee consumed. And the figures of the amounts of the other drugs taken is hair-raising: the antibiotics and painkillers (aspirin for example), medications for varied disorders (from blood thinners to antiarthritic pills), and finally the mood-altering drugs such as tranquilizers and sedatives. Today's teen-agers have grown up in an atmosphere where the message is to trust in drugs to perform magic for all problems—whether for infections or high blood pressure or headaches, or for life's emotional problems and tensions, or simply for social ease.

Telling teen-agers to stop taking drugs or to stop drinking must be reinforced by example. The fat physician puffing at a big cigar who instructs his patients to reduce and stop smoking isn't going to be heeded. No advice will work when it's a matter of "do as I say and not as I do." The authority figure who wants his advice to be followed must set an example that today's already distrustful young people can pattern themselves after.

Alcohol

Suburban youngsters today see fathers rushing home at night, tired and tense, gasping out as soon as they get into the house: "Honey—I'm dying . . . it's been a rough day at the office—I need a drink." Adults' dependence on alcohol conveys a clear message to teen-agers that the best way to deal with one's emotional problems and life's everyday tensions is through the use of drugs.

The problem *is* serious. Dr. Ernest P. Noble, director of NIAAA, says of in-school teen-agers: "Twenty-one percent . . . report consuming five or more drinks per occasion. Nearly 30 percent report getting drunk several times each year [resulting in] impaired school and/or job performance, and accidents." The National Highway Traffic Safety Administration reports nearly eight thousand teen-agers killed annually in accidents involving the use of alcohol. Forty thousand other teen-agers are disfigured.

Explanations for drinking are attributed to rebellious-ness, peer pressure, or simply imitation of adult drinking behavior. Youngsters—like adults—may also drink to gather courage to face life's stresses, to escape from reality, or to forget their worries. Research also points to drinking as part of the process of "anticipatory socialization" in which drinking becomes an indication of entrance into adulthood. Finally, young people in the United States have problems with their drinking simply because they live in a society that itself has problems with alcohol—it's not just the teen-agers' problem, it's everyone's problem. Regular teen-age drinkers usually start at an early age.

Marijuana

The next major drug problem is primarily a youth drug—marijuana. Virtually half the young people under the age of twenty-five use it—but NIDA has found that among those over twenty-five usage drops precipitately. While more than twice as many boys as girls over the age of eighteen have used it, among the twelve to seventeen year olds the boys number only slightly over a third more. Usage among adolescents continues to rise, while that among our general population has remained unchanged since 1975.

What is most disturbing is the evidence of a shift toward the use of higher-potency cannabis (the scientific name for the marijuana plant). One type of cannabis—hashish—is now widely available in the United States. Nearly a third of the eighteen to twenty-five year olds have used hashish, while fewer than one-tenth of those aged twelve to seventeen have. In hashish there is as much as 10 percent THC (tetrahydrocannibinol, the chemical believed to produce the effects of hashish and marijuana) compared to the 1 or 2 percent THC in the typical reefer or marijuana cigarette.

At this time there is no satisfactory idea of what risk is involved in the use of either marijuana or hashish. The answer may become clearer when the far stronger hashish becomes more common. Laboratory tests have shown some evidence of the adverse effects of marijuana on the body's immune response (the system that prevents infection), on basic cell metabolism, and on certain sex hormones such as testosterone and estrogen. Almost nothing is known about the effects of marijuana on persons with chronic disorders (heart patients, for example, or those with psychological impairments).

Dr. Sidney Cohen, University of California professor of psychiatry and a leading international expert on marijuana, summed up the marijuana situation today: "Marijuana is a youth drug, perhaps because of its symbolic aspects—that it is anti-establishment and therefore a drug to smoke whether you like it or not. It has an effect that many young people today relish—distancing one's self from life's problems and the disagreeable aspects of existence, a drug in which you can withdraw mentally and enjoy a sort of reverie state, a fantasy-laden condition." But there is a dangerous side, one that not many people generally recognize but that concerns the experts like Dr. Cohen: "When young people use marijuana as a way of dealing with life, as a means of coping with the stresses and strains of existence, they are thereby deprived of learning other techniques of coping and remain in a sort of perpetual adolescence. They never grow up emotionally—and this can be disastrous to those kids who use marijuana to the exclusion of other devices to deal with the harshness of current existence."

Cigarettes

Teen-agers are also involved in another addiction—cigarette smoking. A late 1975 study of the National Cancer Institute and the American Cancer Society revealed that almost exactly half of all teen-age girls have turned to smoking (in a sharp increase from the past). Slightly more than half the teen-age boys are smoking. The reasons seem in general to be the same as those involved in their drinking and smoking marijuana.

For boys cigarette smoking ties in with masculinity and adulthood, and helps relieve social uneasiness. For girls the marked change is very much a part of their sex's new adolescent attitudes. In both sexes the rejection of authority, the emphasis on the irrational and the emotional, and the accentuated desire for immediate self-fulfillment are factors. And for girls in particular, peer pressure (most youngsters insist a majority of other teen-agers smoke), the belief that the dangers of smoking are exaggerated, the dislike of hearing about things that are bad for them, and complaints that there is too much regulation of their lives lead to the smoking habit. Some teen-agers like to believe that we are close to a cure for cancer.

Hard Drugs

The use of other drugs varies. LSD has proven to be so dangerous and destructive that experts think this has led to the marked reduction in its use. Sedatives such as barbiturates and tranquilizers are so readily available today that no one really knows how much teen-age abuse there is, but the feeling seems to be that youngsters are turning more to alcohol these days. During the last two years, however, there has been an upsurge in the simultaneous use of Valium and Quaalude (a sedative)—with a resultant increasing incidence of overdosing and traffic accidents. Narcotics—heroin is the most widely used in the United States today—are supposedly falling in popularity, perhaps for the same reason as LSD, namely the dangers involved as compared with the more predictable dangers of alcohol and pot. The use of stimulants such as amphetamines and cocaine (classified as a narcotic under federal law) may also be declining. In any case, as the recent study of polydrug use indicated, teen-agers who use these other drugs are relatively few compared to the numbers using alcohol, marijuana, and tobacco.

PREDICTING ADOLESCENT DRUG ABUSE

Predicting which teen-ager will abuse drugs may enable you to take steps to avert misery. Dr. Richard Jessor, a University of Colorado professor of psychology, has found that the high school adolescent drug user, as compared with the nonuser, consistently placed lower values on achievement and higher values on independence; he tended to be more alienated and critical of society; he was more tolerant of deviance and less tolerant of religion; he was less influenced by his parents than by his friends; and he had a lower academic achievement (lower grade-point average). Nonusers tended to show an opposite pattern—one of relative conventionality and conformity.

Dr. Gene M. Smith, Harvard Medical School psychiatry department, and Charles P. Fogg, Boston University College of Basic Studies, studied a combination of nonusers, marijuana users, and hard drug users in a five-year study of students in grades four to twelve. These investigators found that rebelliousness was the best indicator of future drug use. However, the nonusers exhibited higher grade-point averages, less cigarette smoking, less rebelliousness; they were markedly more hardworking, ambitious, self-reliant, and confident academically, and they liked school. They were rated by their peers as highly obedient, hardworking, orderly, trustworthy, nonsociable, and nonimpulsive. By contrast, those who later became users were rated by their peers as more rebellious, impulsive, and less sensitive to the feelings of others, more sociable, talkative, and outgoing than the nonusers.

And Dr. Denise B. Kandel, a Columbia University professor of public health, concludes: "The single most important factor associated with adolescent illicit drug use (marijuana as well as the other illicit drugs) is the pattern of drug use by the adolescent's best friend. Not only does this variable have the strongest effect when considered alone, but also, especially with respect to marijuana, it has a far stronger effect than any other variable when all other factors are considered simultaneously."

In short, what these studies give us is the average behavior pattern of user and nonuser—it doesn't mean that any one particular youngster will follow this pattern. It simply offers some guidelines. NIDA experts conclude: "Many of the factors which have been found to be related to drug use . . . —low academic performance, rebelliousness, depression or criminal activity—appear more often to precede rather than to follow the use of drugs."

PREVENTING ADOLESCENT DRUG ABUSE

In general, the experts aren't nearly as disturbed by the whole drug problem as is the public, and some even feel that the United States is suffering more from a craze of trying to suppress the drug problem than from the problem itself. Some experts feel that we should accept the fact that drug experimentation by teen-agers is a phase of adolescent testing and will be given up as they mature, to be replaced by the establishment's own drugs: alcohol and nicotine.

Handling drug abuse starts in earliest childhood, when parents should establish open communication. An honest heart-to-heart talk with your teen-ager, in which you frankly admit your own feelings and failings, may challenge him to do the same and lay the basis for a whole new understanding. But be a parent and not a pal—don't smoke marijuana, as one father did, so he could talk to his son on a knowing basis. Your teen-ager will respect you much more if you stick to your beliefs openly and honestly and give sound reasons for them. Always show respect for your children while you point out any errors in their thinking, or admit fallacies in your own.

Most of all, a good example is needed—not smoking, not drinking or taking drugs (except for medical reasons) will do more than all the lectures in the world. But don't try to kid the youngster into believing the tranquilizers you take are any more necessary than his marijuana. Problems must be faced openly and the stresses of daily living dealt with on a realistic basis, not avoided with drugs.

If your teen-ager has a drug problem, consult a psychiatrist who is particularly interested in young people. Your child's adolescent physician should be able to recommend a competent professional. It's easier to spot an alcoholic, because drunkenness is more obvious, but drug taking may show itself in personality changes and in functioning at home, in school, or on the job. Drugs tend to enhance defensive, hostile reactions such as lack of patience, quick temper, abusive language. The predictive factors we discussed may alert you to possible danger. But don't take the line one father followed: "Thank God he's not into drugs—he only gets plastered."

Here are some suggestions from experts. Dr. Jared Tinklenberg, a Stanford University professor of psychiatry and a marijuana investigator, feels we must look at the big picture of family relations rather than the too-limited one of drug taking. He urges exploring the total situation: "I don't attach any major importance to the heavy consumption of any one particular drug—the optimal state is not to pollute one's body by ingesting food with many additives or air that's heavily contaminated. My suggestions would focus on the total health standards and life-style of the family, on more total aspects of living, which include not only the avoidance of drugs but also proper nutrition, exercise, rest, and the like. If there's emphasis on health in general, there tends to be less use of drugs; but if parents are smoking heavily, eating inappropriately, drinking excessively, not exercising adequately, always pushing themselves, not getting enough sleep, it's a bit hypocritical to focus on one component of the teen-ager's health, the consumption of drugs."

Knowing the facts and presenting the reality of what we do and do not know about drugs is vital in gaining the respect of your youngster. If you're not sure, say so and explore the answers together. You might well explain your objections to drugs in the terms that Dr. Max Fink, State University of New York professor of psychiatry, uses: "I personally don't use marijuana, but I also don't use alcohol and I don't happen to use tobacco. Anybody who works with brain function measurements finds out quickly that these substances affect the brain rapidly and for long periods—you become sensitive to this, and since the brain is a rather important organ to people like myself, I don't use these substances." Such a rational and realistic approach with its obvious respect for the body and its capacities is the sort of thing that should carry a message on drugs through to your teen-ager.

A good rule of thumb is an old cardinal rule of writing: "Don't say it—show it!" If you do this in your family life and in your relationship with your youngster, you will get much further—dictatorial family or community rules and

laws won't work where teen-agers and drug use are
concerned. Giving the teen-ager elbow room in which to
express and blow off any defiance, and then coming in
with some real proof and information as to why you think
he should or should not do something, is most likely to
keep him from endangering himself with drug experimentation.

Part Two

SPECIAL
PROBLEMS
OF ADOLESCENCE

COMMON COMPLAINTS

ORTHOPEDIC PROBLEMS

PARENTS are often concerned with the way their
children look, and posture contributes to appearance.
Posture results from a host of factors, many of them
emotional. Teen-agers are uncomfortably aware that they
are awkwardly shooting up, often towering above their
friends if they happen to mature faster than their peers. To
this self-consciousness add the admonitions of parents
to "stand up straight," and many teen-agers are certain to
slouch around—shrinking, as it were, from attention. Girls
who develop breasts at an early age may also hunch
forward to hide them. Since few adults have good posture,
the necessary model is missing, and few teen-agers will
believe that posture is important. Many posture problems disappear as teen-agers become more mature, proud

of the way they look, and comfortable with their new bodies.

The rapid growth of the skeleton and slower muscle development during adolescence tend to produce a temporary imbalance, and a relative weakness and awkwardness that the normal growth process automatically brings into balance. The teen-ager who is very active in sports rarely has a posture problem. The problem is chiefly a subjective one: youngsters are less bothered by their posture than their parents are. Only under very rare circumstances (such as unequal leg length or spinal curvature) is there any health difficulty associated with poor teen-age posture.

The best way to treat poor posture is to get a full-length mirror and hope your teen-ager will look in it and decide he or she looks much better with good posture. If necessary, doctors can readily suggest brief exercises (which may be as simple as pushups for round shoulders, situps for swaybacks), but trying to force teen-agers to correct their posture is both hopeless and counterproductive. Competent physicians will advise remedial measures at the time of the annual checkup if necessary.

In spinal curvature (scoliosis) the spine tilts toward the right or left instead of being straight up and down. It occurs in young teen-agers, with four cases out of five being in girls. Doctors don't really know why or how three-quarters of these cases occur, although they do know it can be genetic. Less often it may be due to cerebral palsy or polio in early childhood, to neurofibromatosis, or to unequal leg-length growth. Most cases are harmless, as the abnormal curvature often self-corrects by compensatory opposite curvature of a different spinal level, but it can be crippling and it should be brought to a doctor's attention. Scoliosis requires medical supervision of progression for six months up to two years; severe cases may require surgery or braces.

Another problem (less common than scoliosis but one also chiefly affecting girls) is adolescent kyphosis (humpback or round shoulders). Here there is an obvious roundback deformity with shoulders, head, and neck thrust forward, swayback, and protruding abdomen. More than half these youngsters suffer with persistent back pain. Prompt medical attention is called for when such a development is noticed. Treatment may vary from simple exercises to braces or casts until the growth of the spine has been completed, so that permanent deformity can be prevented.

Another not uncommon orthopedic disorder in adolescents is a condition like tendinitis, which is called Osgood-Schlatter's disease (after its discoverers). This appears as pain below the knee and is a disease of the tibial tubercle (the bony protuberance below the knee), which becomes painful on running or jumping and is tender to the touch. Doctors can diagnose it with a simple office examination, but sometimes X-rays are needed. Treatment varies from avoidance of all sports to wearing a knee brace for six weeks or more. Only occasionally does this disorder affect both legs.

More serious than this disease, but fortunately less common, is a disorder called *slipped capital femoral epiphysis.*

More common in boys than in girls, in blacks than in whites, the disease affects victims who tend to be overweight, to be tall for their age, and to have a slower skeletal maturation. The cause is unknown, but the problem is a disease of the head or end of the femur (the thigh bone where it meets the hip bone). It occurs at the time of the adolescent growth spurt at about the ages of twelve to fifteen in boys and ten to thirteen in girls. It begins insidiously with mild discomfort in the lower third of the thigh, with considerable pain, leg stiffness, and limping after some weeks or months. Your doctor will insist on immediate rest and perhaps even traction. Treatment may also involve surgery to lock the head of the femur in position with a metal insert to align the bone properly.

FATIGUE

The call for an appointment from a young boy's mother was typical: "Doctor, he just seems too tired to drag himself around the house." The adolescent's physician talked with the boy about his school football team and tennis: the supposedly listless youngster became animated and excited. He was obviously deeply involved in vigorous physical activities away from home. The real problem, soon exposed, was a family argument over whether the boy should be allowed to try out for the baseball team or whether he should concentrate solely on his studies. Once the conflict was resolved with an agreement by which the boy was permitted to try out for the team in return for more effort put into his studies, the fatigue disappeared. Fatigue is usually a symptom of an adolescent emotionally distraught or overburdened by his problems (familial, scholastic, extracurricular). Fatigue is easily diagnosed by a concerned, knowledgeable doctor.

More rarely, fatigue can also be a symptom of a wide spectrum of illnesses ranging from very minor to major. When a teen-ager shows fatigue, a prompt medical examination is warranted unless the knowing parent can deal with some conflict behind the symptom and see the fatigue lift immediately and totally. But when there is *any* doubt whatsoever, a medical checkup is essential for the well-being of the youngster.

PROBLEMS OF IMMUNIZATION

In January 1977, Massachusetts suffered the first high school outbreak of measles since 1966. Forty-seven cases occurred in students from thirteen to eighteen years of age. The problem lay to a considerable extent in the fact that the measles vaccines used before 1966 and given to children before the age of fifteen months are of limited efficacy. To compound the problem, most of the youngsters in the Massachusetts school had only an uncertain history of immunization. Because many youngsters during the ages of eight to seventeen do not see doctors, a serious lapse in immunization levels develops. It is important that parents review their children's immunizations with their doctor. Teen-agers between the ages of fourteen and sixteen should have the combined tetanus and diphtheria toxoid immunization (TD). Teen-agers who received a measles vaccine before fifteen months of age should get a booster. Although the mumps vaccine appears to confer lifelong immunity, the rubella (German measles) vaccination is now being questioned. Youngsters getting rubella vaccines currently in use may require a booster dose that will provide lifelong immunity. This is of particular importance to girls and should be provided before twelve years of age because of the terrible damage German measles in a pregnant mother can do to her unborn child. Even youngsters who were adequately immunized in childhood with the "triple baby shots" for diphtheria, pertussis (whooping cough), and tetanus should get the adult TD shots. If any of the childhood shots (for polio, for example) were missed, a thorough consultation with your doctor is essential to obtain proper vaccinations and protection.

PROTECTING TEEN-AGERS IN SPORTS

A greater emphasis has recently been placed on athletics than ever before—and teen-agers are involved in every aspect from unorganized sports at school to varsity teams. Girls demand equal activities now too, and many parents wonder whether girls can compete on a safe basis with boys.

Obviously, any youngster with a chronic disease, such as diabetes or arthritis, should have his athletic activities planned in careful consultation with his physician. The situation should also be reexamined regularly. Limiting activity is a serious problem in adolescents because of the intense anger they develop at any suggestion of control, any order, any feeling of difference from their peers. Careful, sensitive handling is necessary when limits must be imposed on teen-agers or when special exercises must be followed.

Physicians protect adolescents by warning when examinations reveal weaknesses, illnesses, or disorders that preclude certain types of sports. They may suggest exercises to strengthen muscles, for example, or give advice on safe sports or necessary individual precautions, since even the weekend athletes today indulge much more vigorously than ever before.

You might learn from suggestions of the new specialists in sports medicine. You can protect your child by insisting that he or she participate in school athletics only if qualified medical supervision is available. The lack of such proper medical care caused the death of a fifteen-year-old high school athlete who died of heat stroke on the first day of team practice in the summer of 1975. Properly trained coaches and trainers know how to prevent heat stroke and how to treat it. Unless youngsters are fully acclimated, through warm-ups and pre-training, they shouldn't try anything strenuous during the middle of a summer day. Exercise should usually be done in the early morning and late evening when the sun and heat are less intense. Drinking plenty of water before, during, and after exercising is necessary.

Sports are wonderful when they are safe. The safety of

school sports can be assured by making the physician's authority absolute, making his or her decision to sideline a player irreversible. A school district with some forty thousand students in a half-dozen high schools usually has only a single physician to do examinations. Physicians should be involved in checking equipment too, because hand-me-downs that don't fit, or have worn-out areas, are as bad as no equipment at all. Boys have actually lost kidneys because they didn't have proper equipment. Only parents, as citizens and taxpayers, can ensure that their child's school protects its athletes so that they will be sufficiently guarded by adequate physicians, coaches, and other personnel, and have proper equipment. An early consultation with your teen-ager's doctor is a wise precaution before permitting him or her to plan any athletic programs. Common injuries such as torn shoulders in swimmers, wrist, footbone, and ankle fractures in contact sports, and shin splints in runners are not too serious, although muscle tears may require surgery. Any suspected fracture or painful sprain should be X-rayed. Accidents do happen, but sports can be safe and healthy pastimes. Girls need not fear involvement in sports. They can be as aggressive as boys; they have equal endurance and certainly a comparable competitive drive. We see no valid reason why girls shouldn't wrestle or play football or participate in basketball or soccer against boys or in mixed teams. However, before you allow your daughter to be involved in bodily contact competitive sports, particularly with boys, consult her doctor for his approval and advice.

EYE PROBLEMS

Clear, sharp vision is a physical matter: the ability of the lens and the cornea to focus light rays precisely on the onionskin-thick retina at the back of the eye where nerve cells are located to record incoming images and send them back to the brain for interpretation. Should the eyeball be too long or the lens or cornea curvature too great, light rays come to a focus not on the retina but in front of it, and so distant objects will be blurred, although the near ones are clear. This condition is called myopia or nearsightedness. Should the eyeball be too short or the cornea and lens not curved enough, the opposite happens: the light rays are focused behind the retina, and near objects are blurred but distant ones are clear. This is called hyperopia or far-sightedness. Should the curvature of the cornea (the clear, transparent, dime-size cover of the front of the eye) be imperfect, a horizontal, vertical, or oblique distortion of the entire image strikes the retina, and all objects will look warped or distorted. This is called astigmatism.

Actually all these variations of sight occur in perfectly normal eyes and are not considered "abnormal"—they are simply physical variations similar to differences in height. But variations that occur in the eye affect how clearly people see, and they have to be corrected with lenses of some sort. Myopia, for example, is rare at birth and usually only appears at six or eight years of age. It progresses rapidly for a few years and then stabilizes for a while. During adolescence, changes may occur so rapidly that new corrective lenses may be needed every six months or so. This is nothing to be alarmed about, because after the age of twenty little change may occur for the next twenty years. Farsightedness and astigmatism are likely to follow a similar pattern.

There is no scientific evidence that reading in a bad light or in strange positions is likely to affect myopia, farsightedness, or astigmatism. Nor is there any medically acceptable proof that "eye exercises" or special lenses or anything else will change these conditions. Like the adolescents' other growth patterns, the rate or degree of these ocular changes cannot be altered by any measures doctors or adolescents or parents can take, but they do stabilize when the youngster finally reaches physical maturity.

These conditions cannot be "cured"; people who have them must wear corrective lenses the rest of their lives in order to see clearly. Although going without lenses will not harm the eyes, it can endanger the youngster's safety while walking in traffic, riding a bicycle, driving a car, playing ball, or whatever. However, most ophthalmologists agree that teen-agers who have only a slight astigmatism need not wear glasses all the time, but only when reading, watching TV and movies, or when using their eyes at similar fixed distances, as when in school or working on a hobby.

Ophthalmologists in general also prefer glasses simply because a contact lens is a foreign object in the eye and a potential source of irritation. Any decision on the use of contacts should be made in a three-way conference between parent, youngster, and ophthalmologist. There are hard and soft lenses (with different advantages and disadvantages), and before long there may be contacts that can be worn for months without removal.

BRACES

Orthodontia is a protective and preventive measure; it should, however, be utilized with a great deal more hesitation than it is now. Orthodontia has been overused, with no thought given to the problems it may possibly create.

Orthodontia is most likely to be performed in the early teens at precisely the time when a youngster is fighting to break free of all restraints. When a teen-ager, striving to be free, suddenly finds himself bound by various oral appliances and forced to submit to frequent and painful dental procedures, he may rebel by failing to cooperate fully and so inhibit orthodontia's very purpose. By causing teen-agers to concentrate on their mouths, braces create the serious risk of grinding, clenching, and subsequent loosening of the teeth, as well as of gum conditions and tension headaches.

To reduce these risks, parents and teen-ager should question the necessity for braces. They should ask whether the teeth are crooked enough to cause embarrassment or to affect appearance. Orthodontists must decide whether the alignment is so bad that it will cause problems later on. Parents should consult with a general dentist who has nothing to gain from orthodontia. Unless there is a physical or emotional reason for orthodontia, it should not be undertaken. Orthodontia for minor cosmetic reasons only should be avoided.

Routine dental care is certainly called for throughout adolescence. Widespread fluoridation of water supplies has recently improved the chances of avoiding dental decay, but regular care is vital to oral health.

Eight

THE CHRONIC DISEASES

MEDICAL care of the adolescent is always a problem because most active, growing young people are so independent and antiauthority that any medical instructions or limitations, any necessary health regimens that doctors set, have roughly the same effect that a waving red flag has on an angry bull. Even at the expense of their health, many teen-agers will ignore health care. The chronic diseases teen-agers may suffer are a special problem, because they call for long-term acceptance of being different from peers, of limitations at a time when the teen-agers are trying to throw off restrictions.

ARTHRITIS

"I guess I was thirteen when it started. There was this excruciating pain and swelling of the joints in both feet and my left shoulder. It got to the point I couldn't put on my shoes, and my arm froze in an upright position. . . . I had to drop out of sports, and couldn't get a job like the rest of the kids. . . . You lose all your self-confidence. . . . You just withdraw from things." This is how one young victim of juvenile rheumatoid arthritis (JRA) recalls his initial bout with the dread arthritis of the young. It emphasizes the problems arthritis creates for the teen-ager: the limitations, the giving up of being with peers, the loss of self-esteem, finally the withdrawal. This disease can be a disaster in its impact on the adolescent. More crippling than the pain, the suffering, and the joint changes is the devastating psychological effect on the teen-ager's emotional development.

Unfortunately, there is no miracle drug, no magic cure, for JRA. We depend today on total management rather than any single treatment. Specialists called rheumatologists are available for consultation, but even these experts are not fully agreed on whether JRA is a separate and distinct disease entity or just another form of the well-known rheumatoid arthritis of the adult. In any case, JRA includes those rheumatoid arthritic disorders that strike before the age of sixteen, afflicting more girls than boys, and varying greatly in pattern. The complexities of JRA make its diagnosis a matter of clinical judgment often arrived at by eliminating the other arthritic disorders.

JRA in about a third of the cases may begin mildly and affect only a few joints or even one joint (most often the knee). That and other joints later become more painful, swollen, and stiff. In one-third of these patients an eye problem develops as a late complication. Another third to one-half of JRA patients have multiple joints involved from the start, usually bilaterally and in both small and large joints. In about one-fourth of JRA patients disease may be heralded by a high, intermittent fever (as much as 105°), an evanescent skin rash, spleen enlargement, and minimal signs of arthritis. The arthritis eventually involves large and small joints in this type of JRA known as Still's Disease. Half the children affected become retarded in their growth and development during the active period of the disease, but when it enters a period of remission or is controlled by medical care, the youngster's growth resumes and may eventually be normal. If the disorder is long-lasting, it may retard sexual maturation as well. Aspirin is the mainstay of all JRA therapy, but when it fails, steroids or even gold injections may be tried. What is most upsetting to the teen-ager is the occasional need for splints and similar devices, as well as special regular exercises to prevent deformity and maintain muscle strength.

The outlook for JRA, however, is usually quite good, and the disorder often has spontaneous remissions, leaving little or no damage to the youngster. About three out of four JRA victims have normal or near-normal joint function by adulthood. The outlook is poorest when the condition strikes between the ages of ten and fourteen, and when it starts in the small joints of the body rather than the large ones such as knees or hips or elbows.

A variety of arthritic conditions can sometimes affect teen-agers, but they are not common enough to warrant discussion here, except for one increasingly common form—gonococcal arthritis. It is often the first sign of VD and it strikes about 3 percent of untreated gonorrhea victims. Actually, gonococcal arthritis has become the most frequent form of infectious arthritis. It's a medical emergency with joint inflammation, pain, palpable heat, and perhaps fever. Treatment must be immediate, because joint destruction can be devastatingly swift; however, cure (with penicillin or other antibiotics) has been almost 100 percent and response to treatment is rapid. The adolescent who complains of pain of any kind—and in arthritis the first symptom is likely to be pain, joint swelling, or stiffness—should be brought to a doctor.

DIABETES

A mother noticed that her fourteen-year-old daughter was suddenly drinking enormous amounts of fluid (water, soda, "anything that was wet, even handfuls of snow") and going to the bathroom in a steady parade (even during the night). Eating enormous amounts of food, the child was still losing weight; she was listless and unusually irritable, and the quality of her school work deteriorated. Such a story demonstrates the diagnosis, diabetes, which is proven by blood and urine tests.

Diabetes (technically diabetes mellitus, sugar diabetes) is a disorder which cannot be cured, but it can be managed so that the victim can live a virtually normal life. However, its impact on a teen-ager can be disastrous, because it demands careful attention to a fairly strict diet, regular, very exact amounts of self-injected insulin, and exercise with sufficient rest. Because of the teen-ager's need to be independent, such restrictions are a problem—no going out with the gang for hamburgers, no staying up until two A.M., no experimenting with that first drink, regular injections at special times. The need for some of these restrictions is being hotly debated by doctors today, and a youngster's physician is the one to decide on the correct regimen.

Some physicians say that the psychological problems of the teen-age diabetic are the predominant difficulties in the treatment of this condition. All the things that teen-agers want to do are off-limits to young diabetics, and they rebel at this far more than younger or older sufferers. They deny the fact that they have a disease, try to prove to the world that they can fit in with their healthy peers, and as a result their illness becomes erratic and makes these years particularly difficult.

Diabetes starting before adolescence delays menarche or puberty. In fact, many of the toughest problems of diabetes occur when the disease appears just before or during adolescence. Teen-agers need a lot of support in the face of psychological conflict about body image, maturity, and growing up, and this confusion in turn causes trouble with diabetes. A diabetic teen-ager's insulin requirements frequently increase with his growth spurt—and this frightens the youngster, because he thinks the disease is getting worse. An increased need for insulin at this time is normal, however. After they pass adolescence and calm down, many teen-agers have lower insulin requirements and do very well. The hormonal changes in girls make managing their diabetes more difficult than in boys.

Diabetes is a relatively frequent problem among adolescents under the age of sixteen. The disease usually appears suddenly in teen-agers, with weight loss, frequent urination, and excessive thirst. It is a disease in which a deficiency of insulin (a hormone secreted by the pancreas) interferes with the body's ability to properly utilize sugars (carbohydrates). If diabetes is untreated, the excessive sugar in the bloodstream combined with the failure to use it properly by metabolizing tissue cells puts stress on fat metabolism. This leads to excessive ketones in the blood and decreases blood bicarbonate, a condition called *acidosis*. Occasionally, only a few days of illness may lead to severe acidosis and even coma. Characteristically, for the first few weeks or months after initial treatment, insulin requirements drop. But stress can precipitate acidosis and excessive blood sugar levels.

A diabetic teen-ager should have a doctor who is familiar with the problems of both adolescents and diabetes. Often the adolescent's own physician will be best able to manage the child with the backing of a specialist, a diabetologist, or of a general endocrinologist, who sees the youngster at the start and begins the management of the disease. That is then taken over by the child's own physician, who calls on the expert whenever advice is needed.

Doctors today tend to use the minimum restrictions necessary to keep this disease under control. Management is difficult, for the youngster must learn to use complex dietary tables to juggle his food so he gets what he needs, making allowances for dietary alterations (when he goes out with friends) and so on. Doctors try to keep life as normal as possible for the diabetic by encouraging exercise and sports, but the teen-ager must learn to work closely with his doctor and accept the necessary restrictions and requirements, such as taking his insulin shots regularly.

URINARY TRACT INFECTIONS

Fortunately, since kidneys are essential to life, kidney problems are relatively rare in teen-agers. The kidneys process nearly two thousand quarts of blood a day, monitor its contents, filter it, and cleanse it of all impurities. If they stop working, an artificial kidney (dialysis) is used as a last-ditch life-saving measure. Kidney transplants are the only truly successful organ transplants. The longest-lasting kidney transplant is now more than twenty years old; and it is still working perfectly in an Oklahoma housewife, whose twin donated her kidney. Kidney transplants are now being performed at a rate of more than two thousand a year.

The most common kidney problem is infection (pyelonephritis), which is carried to the kidney by bacteria either borne in the bloodstream or working their way up through the ureters (tubes carrying urine down from the kidneys to the bladder). In one-third of these conditions the infection first shows itself as a frequent urge to urinate, with a burning or scalding sensation, chills and fever, loin pain, stomach ache, vomiting, nausea, and general malaise. Prompt and expert medical care with current antibiotic drugs is essential to keep this acute infection from turning into a long-lasting chronic one.

The most common urinary tract disorder, however, is

cystitis, an infection of the urinary bladder. It is rare enough in boys to indicate some structural or other abnormality if it occurs. In adult women, cystitis is common, but it is rare in young girls (only 5 percent contract it). However, for the last half century or so, doctors have been talking of "honeymoon cystitis"—a simple bladder infection that frequently occurs in young women following their first sexual intercourse. Since young women are having sex earlier and earlier these days, cystitis must be anticipated in any teen-age girl. The condition, however, is usually harmless when treated promptly, although it may be intensely painful. It causes a terrible urgency to urinate frequently (often with only a little urine passed). The urine may be bloody as well. Chills and fever, nausea, and pain in the back may all appear. Precisely why this condition should follow the first intercourse in women is a mystery. Treatment is initiated after obtaining a urine analysis and culture. A sulfa drug (such as Gantrisin) or ampicillin or cephalexin will be given for ten to fourteen days, although treatment is not always successful and many drugs may need to be tried. Cystitis recurs.

Another not uncommon problem of teen-age boys and girls is proteinuria, protein or albumin in the urine. Most of these asymptomatic cases are actually functional, resulting from fever, upper respiratory infection, exposure to heat or cold, or even previous exercise. Repetition of urine analysis a week or two later might determine the cause. The majority of cases of proteinuria in otherwise healthy adolescents is due to his or her standing upright all day. It is called orthostatic proteinuria, and it's nothing serious. It may be diagnosed by repeating a urine analysis on a morning specimen which the teen-ager has voided after resting in bed ten minutes after awakening. This specimen will usually not show the protein, and parents as well as teen-agers may be reassured.

One of the most common complaints of young females seeking medical advice is vaginal discharge. This is often accompanied by symptoms of mild-to-severe itching or vaginal burning, perineal odor, vulvar swelling, tenderness, and difficult and/or frequency of urination, although vaginal discharge can occur without these symptoms. The causative agents may be either *Hemophilus vaginalis* (a bacterium), Trichomonas infestation (a parasite), or *Candida albicans* (Monilia or yeast infection). Discharge varies slightly with each of these causes, and a few simple laboratory tests will usually identify the specific causative organism. Yeast infection is the most common of the vaginitides. It is treated with miconazole vaginal cream, clotrimazole vaginal tablets, or nystatin vaginal tablets inserted nightly for one or two weeks. The Trichomonas is treated with metronidazole or a vaginal cream (AVC cream). Hemophilus infection may be treated with a triple sulfa cream for two weeks or oral triple sulfa tablets for ten days. When, in rare cases, the latter don't work, oral ampicillin four times a day for seven days will usually clear the infection.

These disorders are caused by improper hygiene and can be aggravated by wearing tight pants. Cotton underpants and cleanliness are the most useful preventive measures.

ALLERGIES

Allergies are of major medical importance in adolescents, but few—except for an occasional asthma—actually begin in the teen years. Allergies that plague adolescents include hay fever, allergic rhinitis (its symptoms are similar to those of hay fever, although it is not caused by pollen), eczema, nasal polyps, and hives. Many of these allergies precede or accompany bronchial asthma. Treatment today is with medications and desensitization, "allergy shots."

Asthmatic girls outnumber boys. Both boys and girls show allergies to aspirin and other simple chemicals. Those who first get asthma in early childhood often appear to "grow out of it" in adulthood, but those who first become asthmatics in their teens may often suffer permanent, persistent, and severe asthma, requiring bronchodilator drugs and even steroids. Diet and activity are not restricted, but avoiding house dust by using filters and getting rid of dust collectors such as carpets is of the utmost importance to both asthmatics and allergic rhinitis sufferers. Some hay fever or allergic rhinitis sufferers do well with the occasional use of nose drops and sprays or oral medicines, although some require desensitization. Nasal polyps might require surgical removal even though they still may grow back. An electronic precipitator in the vent system may help to reduce dust and allergies. Breathing exercises for asthmatics give no significant long-term improvement but using the diaphragm muscles and breathing against pursed lips does help during an attack, and similar results can be attained by singing lessons when well. A newly discovered phenomenon among adolescents today has recently appeared. Known as EIA or EIB, these are exercise-induced asthma or exercise-induced bronchospasm. The patient is troubled by coughing or wheezing, which is totally reversible and of short duration, but which builds in intensity within fifteen minutes after moderately strenuous exercise. It then peaks and self-terminates, but it can be quite frequent and distressing to the adolescent, especially after running, soccer, basketball, or football. Cooler temperatures and lower humidity of inhaled air seem to increase the chances of EIA occurring. Treatment consists of physical conditioning and prophylactic medications. Avoidance of the activity that precipitated EIA is a last resort only in cases resisting all other therapies. Swimming, by the way, is tolerated very well by teen-agers prone to EIA.

Nine

HIGH-RISK DISEASES

CANCER

THE very word *cancer* strikes fear into the hearts and minds of human beings, and for many parents it is virtually unthinkable—but there is truly good news today! For the first time in humanity's long struggle against disease it is possible to speak of cancer in terms of cure. True, the cures are limited to certain cancers (malignant tumors or *malignancies*), but even conservative experts now use the word "cure" where certain select malignancies are concerned. In fact, Dr. Donald Pinkel, pediatrician at Milwaukee's Medical College of Wisconsin, titled his 1976 article in the conservative *Journal of the American Medical Association* "Curability of Childhood Cancer."

Cancer is today the most common disease killer of children from one to fifteen years of age and the second cause of all deaths in this age range (accidents alone cause more young deaths than cancer). In ten to nineteen year olds, cancer causes roughly one-quarter of all medically related deaths. Among cancers that occur in the teen years, acute leukemia and other blood and lymphatic malignancies (such as Hodgkin's disease) are by far the most common killers, with cancers of the brain and the nervous system second and those of bone a close third.

Acute leukemia is by far the most fatal of cancers, but its prognosis has been turned around dramatically. Acute lymphatic leukemia (ALL), the most frequent form of childhood cancer, was almost always fatal ten years ago. In November 1965 a boy in his late teens was brought into Roswell Park Memorial Institute (New York State's unique comprehensive cancer center in Buffalo). He was too sick to walk and had to be carried to a wheelchair. After two weeks of chemotherapy—the treatment of cancer by drugs and chemicals—this boy was not only walking but was also discharged from the hospital, although at first he returned weekly for treatments, and then every other week. Before long he was able once more to lead an active teen-age life, including delivering newspapers over a two-and-a-half mile rural route on foot or bicycle. In May of 1972 he was taken off the anticancer drugs, and as Dr. Arnold I. Freeman, associate chief cancer research pediatrician at Roswell Park, put it: "Today we can say he appears cured. . . . He personifies the great strides made by cancer researchers in so short a time."

The use of chemotherapy and radiotherapy (X-rays and other forms of radiation), as Dr. Pinkel points out, has been combined in all patients to keep approximately half of the children stricken with the disease free of all evidence of this cancer. About 80 percent of these victims have remained free of this cancer after *all* treatment had been stopped for periods of time up to ten years.

Hodgkin's disease was once 75 percent fatal in children and adolescents, but now, Dr. Pinkel reports, combined chemotherapy and radiotherapy have produced lengthy disease-free survival in 80 percent of the youngsters with this disease. Dr. Henry S. Kaplan, director of Stanford University's cancer biology research laboratory, summarizes the situation: "Hodgkin's disease can indeed be permanently cured, and continuing advances in its diagnosis and treatment have brought us within sight of the total therapeutic conquest of this once inexorably fatal malady." There is hope now also for such feared bone cancers as osteogenic sarcoma (osteosarcoma), where only amputation of the leg successfully cured some 20 percent of victims. Intensive chemotherapy following surgery now offers new hope that only the future can prove or disprove.

The American public was shocked a few years ago to learn that the teen-age son of one of our most prominent political families lost a leg to a bone tumor. Osteosarcoma, for some unknown reason, is more common in boys. Most people, however, are unaware that tumors of the ovaries are actually not uncommon in teen-age girls, and the risk increases as they get older. These ovarian tumors are most often found on routine physical examinations (another reason for annual checkups), for they are usually without symptoms, although occasionally they do cause pain and even nausea or vomiting. The prognosis for ovarian cancer is quite good if the ovaries are removed.

It has been found that the best results with cancers are obtained at centers that specialize in cancer problems—specialized children's hospitals, university hospitals with special pediatric oncology (cancer) services, and the major cancer centers. Although these centers are not available everywhere, your doctor knows the names and locations of the best and nearest centers.

Handling the adolescent with cancer is one of the ultimate tests of a physician. It calls for the coordinated efforts of the youngster's own doctor, the oncologist, and other highly specialized experts. Parents should be told when there is cancer and what the exact nature of the disease is. They should also be given an honest explanation of the proposed treatment. The teen-ager too should be told about his condition if he wishes to know.

Adolescents with cancer need advice, support, and help. They need knowledgeable answers to their questions about life expectancy, school, future career plans, sports, sexual activity, even about eventual marriage. They should be encouraged to participate in decisions on treatment—surgery and any question of amputation; chemotherapy, which may involve experimental drugs; and even on the stopping of therapy. The youngster should have the comfort, warmth, and support at all times of a concerned, involved physician.

HEART CONDITIONS

Doctors use stethoscopes to hear the sounds made by the blood as it rushes into and out of the chambers of the heart, as the heart valves that control this flow open and close. The inlet and outlet valves swing open and shut at the same time, sounding like a pair of double doors slamming shut. If these valves are damaged (say from rheumatic fever), the openings are narrowed and the blood rushing through makes a roaring sound. If a valve leaks and the blood regurgitates, flowing back instead of forward, it produces a different sound. Such prolonged, abnormal sounds during the heart cycle are called *murmurs*, and there are dozens of different kinds. It's possible for today's cardiologists (heart specialists) to utilize modern electronic devices to time the "splitting of a heart sound" (the time between each valve's opening or closing) to within one or two hundredths of a second. Such tiny differences may make important diagnoses possible.

Chest pains in adolescents, particularly in boys, are also common, and only rarely due to heart disease. One of the most common causes is simply strained rib muscles, but chest pain is often caused by fear. Typically, one sixteen-year-old boy whose father recently had a heart attack came to his doctor in a panic: just before his exams he suddenly experienced chest pains and a need for breathing very deeply to relieve his sudden shortness of breath. He even became dizzy. After intensive examination and tests, his doctor reassured the family that it was only an emotional reaction. However, cases like this aren't always emotional, so a medical checkup is always imperative when symptoms appear, even though less than 5 percent of chest pains are actually due to heart conditions.

Also common during the teen years are the appearance of heart murmurs, most of which are functional, such as those caused by sudden growth and the resulting altered anatomic relationship between the changing heart size and shape and that of the chest in which the heart lies. Murmurs in teen-agers are certainly no cause for panic, but they should be carefully investigated by the youngster's physician, who may advise a consultation with a cardiologist. The heart specialist may use exercise tolerance tests, special heart examinations called echocardiography (checking heart size and function with ultrasound), perhaps even heart catheterization and angiocardiography (tubes passed into the heart or substances injected to make the heart's blood vessels visible in X-rays). However, the vast majority of heart murmurs in teen-agers are "innocent," and some are thought to come from an increased intensity of the normal vibrations of blood flow in the artery to the lungs. Actually, about a third of all teen-agers may have such innocent murmurs.

Enlarged hearts are now being recognized as normal in young people, for this organ may be materially enlarged in the healthy but highly trained teen-age athlete. There is a new awareness of the importance of exercise for heart disease prevention, but teen-agers' hearts should be carefully checked before they enter competitive sports. And proper exercises should be prescribed by a doctor for youngsters with heart problems.

Rheumatic fever has been called a disease that "nips at the joints but bites the heart." Although markedly less frequent than it once was, the disease is still important, for it can and does produce permanent damage to the heart and its valves, perhaps leaving murmurs. Rheumatic fever typically follows on the heels of a "strep" infection (usually a strep sore throat), but exactly how the bacteria set off rheumatic fever is unclear. Some doctors believe that about half the initial attacks of this disease affect the heart. Prompt medical care and antibiotic therapy can reduce the after-effects of rheumatic fever—heart involvement and the once-feared recurrences—to a minimum.

Rheumatic fever in adolescents is more subtle than in younger children. Only slightly more than half of the teen-agers who have rheumatic fever suffer from a sore throat before the fever. A painful arthritis with slight fever and malaise are the most common symptoms. Treatment includes penicillin for the infection, aspirin for the arthritis, and at least two weeks of bed rest until acute symptoms are gone. When the heart is not involved, a gradual return to normal activity is allowed. However, when the heart is involved, four or more weeks of bed rest are prescribed until the heart becomes normal once again. The school schedule should be limited, with transportation both ways and limited use of stairs. Physical education may only be resumed on the doctor's advice. Penicillin is used pro-phylactically under the doctor's direction. Once the heart has been damaged it may remain that way for life.

HYPERTENSION

High blood pressure is a new area of concern for teen-agers. Certainly every young person should routinely have his blood pressure taken at least once a year. Dr. Sidney Blumenthal, director of the Division of Heart and Vascular

Diseases at the National Heart, Lung and Blood Institute, is particularly knowledgeable in this area and believes that there is reason for concern when a teen-ager's blood pressure is above 140/90, particularly if he comes from a family with a history of hypertension, premature strokes, or heart attacks in those under the age of fifty. Some observers set the range for those twelve to fifteen years of age at 130 to 140/75 to 82 in boys and 75–88 in girls, and consider such youngsters as borderline hypertensives, raising the figures slightly for older teen-agers.

However, only when three separate determinations of blood pressure (done while the youngster is on his back and, say, the second a week after the first and the third a month after the second) are all on a high level, is the youngster regarded as having mild or borderline hypertension. Dr. Blumenthal advises periodic examinations of blood pressure, avoidance of overweight, a very active physical activity program, and avoidance of salt abuse and cigarette smoking. He notes: "All of us take far too much salt, and the average adolescent diet, with its hamburgers, frankfurters, and potato chips, consists of a large amount of salt. Salt should not be eliminated, but it should be taken in moderation. Some doctors also believe everybody should be on a low cholesterol diet, but I don't agree. Only if the blood cholesterol test indicates an unduly high level will I treat the youngster this way."

Treating adolescents is difficult because of their resistance to taking medication, especially when they feel well or when the medication makes them ill. The low-salt diet often prescribed is not usually followed by the teen-age hypertensive. No restrictions on exercises should be imposed for most youngsters, except for those few who are on antihypertensive drugs that cause faintness or dizziness after strenuous exercise.

Girls on the pill must be watched if they have high blood pressure. This is particularly necessary if they have close relatives who suffer from hypertension, or if the girl herself has in the past put on weight during her menses or become puffy because of her tissues filling with fluid.

Some experts find that physical activities vary in their effect on blood pressure. Certain kinds—the rhythmic types such as walking, running, golf, baseball, basketball—actually lower the pressure. But the static exercises such as wrestling or weightlifting, in which the youngster is pushing against a relatively immovable object, increase blood pressure.

Ninety-five percent of cases of hypertension in adolescents are primary—that is, without known cause. The dangers of hypertension increase as the child grows older, so it is best to be vigilant.

Ten

LOW-RISK DISEASES

THESE are the diseases which, though potentially fatal, are rarely so. They are debilitating and cause absence from school for two to four weeks. Most of these diseases are not chronic, but they may be relapsing. They are nuisance illnesses for adolescents.

MONONUCLEOSIS

Infectious mononucleosis ("the kissing disease," "glandular fever," or just plain "mono") is a disease of myth and mystery even though it was first described nearly a century ago in 1889. The disease is due to the so-called Epstein-Barr virus (EBV). It is now thought that EBV triggers an autoimmune disease (one in which a person's own defenses turn on his own tissues and destroy them), particularly in certain teen-agers. This disease results in mono.

It was first suggested that the disease was passed along by deep kissing, but some observers note that its victims rarely report contact with an active case of the disease. Mononucleosis is seldom contracted by roommates, families (blood relatives or spouses), or other close contacts of those sick with the disease. However, there have been reports of the disease appearing over a period of months in various victims, all of whom were exposed to one particular person. It is now believed to be passed along by a carrier (someone who transmits the disease without being actively ill with it). And it seems to take three to seven weeks after the initial exposure for the disease to develop.

While almost anyone at any age can get mono (it's been diagnosed in infants and in octogenarians), as many as 80 percent of the proven cases have appeared in people between the ages of fifteen and thirty. U.S. Public Health Service studies indicate that close to one hundred thousand college students come down with this disease every year. Experts at the National Institute of Allergy and Infectious Diseases (NIAID) say that it "appears" that the disease is more common in males than in females. But like so much else about this mystery disease, this sex differential has never been scientifically proven.

There is no special season for the disease, although college health experts, who have probably studied the disease most intensively, report they see more of it in the fall and the early spring. Some evidence does suggest the mouth and throat to be the route of entry, and coughing and sneezing may also spread the disease. But mono is *not* highly contagious, and there would seem little justification for isolating its victims.

Typically, the victim of mono shows up, as did one nineteen year old, with the statement: "Doc, I think I'm dying—my throat is killing me and everything else hurts too. I'm burning up one minute and having chills the next, my glands are all swollen and I'm so weak I can't drag myself around." This is a good summary of the most common symptoms—and explains why it's regarded as such a terrible disease.

In general, however, physicians find that mono actually is not really a terribly serious disease. About 35 percent of suffering teen-agers miss no more than a week of school, and most of them return to their classes once they are given medication. Doctors in the community who only see an occasional case think it a serious condition only because it looks so bad and because the teen-agers feel so terrible. Experts regard it as a benign disease, because only very rarely are there serious complications that result in death (such as a ruptured spleen, nervous system involvement, or throat blockage). In fact, only eighty-seven deaths from mono were reported in all the medical literature up to 1970. However, two youngsters had such severe throat and larynx swelling that they had to have a tracheotomy to permit breathing until the condition subsided.

The disease usually begins insidiously and vaguely with fatigue, loss of energy, sore throat, and perhaps some slight fever—in various degrees and combinations. Sometimes the disease remains so mild that it's not even recognized and is over without ever being treated. However, mono can start suddenly with shaking chills and severe malaise, bad sore throat, and marked debility and fatigue. Even the acute symptoms, however, are usually over in a week or ten days, and fatigue and loss of pep usually last only two to four weeks.

Virtually all mono victims will have enlarged lymph nodes (glands) in the neck and perhaps elsewhere (especially the upper body); nine out of ten will be tired or weak; four out of five will have a fever (often 102° or more) and a sore throat; half of all victims will have enlarged spleens and about as many will have puffy eyes. A measleslike body rash and jaundice appear in a small number of cases. The whole affair may start suddenly or come on gradually. The disease is a masquerader: its sore throat and other symptoms may resemble a strep throat; swollen lymph nodes may make one think of leukemia, stiff neck of meningitis, abdominal pain of acute appendicitis, even the cough of tuberculosis. However, today doctors can take a few drops of blood and make a quick, simple office test to spot the disease. If the test is negative for a youngster who looks as if he has mono, it will be repeated, because it may take a week or two before it becomes positive. There are other tests as well.

In the past, doctors prescribed four to six weeks of bed rest with limitation of activity for three months after all the symptoms had disappeared, so that mono threatened the loss of a whole semester or even a full year of college. But today, doctors know that the only admonition really necessary is the avoidance of strenuous exercise: the only real hazard of mono is the possibility of damage to the spleen from overexertion. The rest of the treatment is symptomatic, with additional rest and a well-balanced diet. Aspirin is advised for the headache, muscle pains, and chill. Antibiotics are used only in the 10 percent of mono patients with strep sore throat, and steroids are used only in the very rare severe complications.

HEPATITIS

Hepatitis is an inflammation of the liver and can be caused by virus infection or chemical compounds. There are two types of viral hepatitis: serum or Hepatitis B (formerly thought to be transmitted only by infected syringes or injections of blood products) and infectious or Hepatitis A (formerly thought to be contracted only from contaminated food). However, it's now been shown that both A and B can be transmitted by the other's supposed route. Teen-agers are at high risk here because of drug abuse, their carelessness about sanitation and hygiene, and careless use of improperly sterilized instruments for ear or nose piercing or skin tattooing. The life-style of our teen-agers today and their rebelliousness make it very difficult for them to accept the limitations and medical instructions accompanying this disease.

The best-known symptom of hepatitis is the obvious yellow skin color or jaundice, but doctors also look for fever, chills, headache, painful joints, abdominal tenderness, nausea and vomiting, and appetite loss. A striking distaste for cigarette smoke may develop, even if someone else is smoking. Darkened urine and itchiness may precede the jaundice, but as the disease progresses the liver becomes enlarged and tender, the urine cola-colored, stools light-colored, and the spleen enlarged. The symptoms are the same for both Hepatitis A and B. Blood and liver function tests monitor the victim, and most adolescents do recover fully, with jaundice disappearing within two months and full recovery following two to six weeks thereafter. However, the very rare unfortunate victim (only one or two in one hundred) may develop liver failure that can be fatal.

Little today can be done for viral hepatitis. Activity is not limited, and a full diet is offered as long as hepatitis remains uncomplicated during the initial ten days of observation. Hospitalization may be necessary only when the patient is dehydrated, vomiting, or unable to care for himself. Isolation precautions in hospital or at home are advised for the first two to four weeks after the onset. Dietary limitations are only applied to alcohol (none at all!) and doctors check any drugs being taken that might trouble the already damaged liver. Family and teen-ager must take considerable precautions to prevent the healthy from contracting the disease. Gamma globulin injections may be given to people who have been in close contact with Hepatitis A victims during the infectious period before precautions were established. No better example of the highly infectious nature of Hepatitis A can be given than the time it contaminated the water fountains used by the Holy Cross football team, which it struck down with almost 100 percent efficacy in 1969.

Adolescents today can also induce hepatitis in its toxic form by inhaling cleaning solvents (carbon tetrachloride, for example) and imbibing excessive alcohol. Even drugs used for health purposes can cause toxic hepatitis: the pill in certain women, certain antituberculosis drugs or antipsychotic agents, even some anesthetics. Although doctors can quickly diagnose and identify the cause of these conditions, the real problem doctors face is getting the teen-ager to avoid the causes in the future.

Still another type of hepatitis (chronic active hepatitis) occurs during the teen years. It is more common in girls, and no infectious agent has been identified. Its symptoms are similar to Hepatitis A and B, but there is no jaundice in a fifth of its victims. This type of hepatitis is a chronic, life-threatening disease that should be treated at a medical center to assure expert handling of both the disease and the potent medications used for it (steroids, for example). If treatment fails, hepatic coma and death can result.

DIGESTIVE TRACT DISORDERS

Abdominal symptoms—cramps, diarrhea, abdominal tenderness—that recur or last for more than a week or two call for a prompt medical consultation. Rectal bleeding and bloody or black-colored stools are also good reasons to call a doctor. Teen-agers are susceptible to regional enteritis (a curious and still mysterious inflammatory condition of the bowel), which may even interfere with growth and development; and to ulcerative colitis, also of unknown cause.

When long-term medications fail, surgeons today

remove the diseased sections of the intestine so that a teen-ager can afterward live a relatively normal life without having to worry about flareups of these conditions, which impose heavy limitations on the health and freedom that are so important for adolescent maturation.

Peptic or stomach disorders are nearly as common in teen-agers as they are in adults and include a whole range of poorly understood problems leading to heartburn and pain (a boring, dull ache often relieved by food), nausea and vomiting, and even stomach distension. Changes that take place in peptic disorders can lead to ulcers, which are treated in teen-agers the same way as in adults: with antacids, dietary restrictions, and cimetidine, a histamine antagonist.

To make matters worse, many of the drugs young people use are also capable of stirring up peptic problems. Alcohol markedly stimulates stomach acid production as does the caffeine in coffee. Tobacco lowers the local factors in the stomach that provide protection against acid. Treatment is a medical matter, and help should be sought promptly before more serious problems arise. Doctors may use an ulcer diet or special drugs. Psychotherapy may be advisable for some teen-agers.

Psychosomatic disorders can be terribly troubling. The so-called irritable bowel syndrome, for example, can cause constipation or diarrhea, and often severe abdominal pain. Medication is usually not the best approach here because it avoids the only safe, permanent answer for the young victim—learning how to deal with life in a way that will permit him to cope without developing physical symptoms. Psychotherapy may be necessary. Fortunately, young people today accept the idea of a "shrink" much more readily than their parents do.

PNEUMONIA

By far the single most frequent cause of pneumonia in adolescents is a germ called Mycoplasma, the tiniest bacterium known. Epidemics of mycoplasmal pneumonia occur in the United States mostly in the late summer and early fall and strike those in the ten- to nineteen-year-old range more than any other age group. It plays no sex favorites, striking boys and girls equally. Its victims suffer fatigue, headache, and slight cough, fever, and chills.

The youngster with this disease isn't terribly sick and improves within five to eight days, although the disease may sometimes drag on for two weeks. The fatigue and cough, however, can persist for two to four weeks. Antibiotics usually cure this pneumonia in a week or ten days. Adolescents also get viral or other bacterial pneumonias but less commonly than other age groups. Other types of pneumonia take the same course and are treated the same in everybody.

TUBERCULOSIS

Although tuberculosis has ceased to be a major adolescent health problem and treatment has become very effective, it nevertheless is still a disease to be reckoned with. Infection with the tubercle bacillus has become more common in the teen years, although the prevalence of the actual disease has decreased: it is possible to be infected with this germ and yet not have the disease known as tuberculosis with its lung, bone, and other organ destruction. High hormone levels seem to make teen-agers aged twelve to fifteen more susceptible, but why teen-agers are prone to tuberculosis is not clear. TB is contracted from another person who has an active case of it. Foamites spewed by coughing are the infecting agents.

The teen-ager may have no symptoms at all or only a very slight fever, cough, or increased fatigue, or he may simply have an unusual number of respiratory infections. Simple tests are available, and testing should be done annually, but unfortunately this is not a practice in most American communities today.

Sanatarium care, hospitalization, and bed rest for this disease are virtually obsolete. Proper treatment includes adequate rest and nutrition (usually with a high-protein and high-calcium diet). Moderate exercise, including swimming, is encouraged, but competitive sports may be restricted for some months. Blood tests should be done every three or four months, as well as chest X-rays at intervals determined by the severity of the disease. The problems of the disease and the outlook for the future must be explained to both teen-ager and parents. It is important to know whether there has simply been some low-grade infection with this bacterium or whether the bacterium is causing the active disease. Thus any need to take antibacterial medication for one year for the active disease, or to prevent the low-grade infection from turning into the active disease, will be clearer to and more readily accepted by the patient.

Eleven

PROBLEMS WITH FOOD

IN every rapidly growing young person the role of food—nutrition and its necessary elements—is obviously essential and a source of great concern to many parents.

OBESITY

When obesity affects 30 to 40 percent of all Americans, when it is a major factor in shortening life span, a breeder of diseases, and a source of serious unhappiness, then there is sufficient reason to regard it as *the* major American health problem today. The exact incidence of this condition is not entirely clear, nor is its definition, but in general the adult who is twenty pounds or more overweight can be considered obese—as are 30 percent of men and 40 percent of women. Studies have shown conclusively that the obese suffer higher death rates from heart disease, stroke, diabetes, and a host of other diseases. Simply reducing overweight can reduce blood cholesterol (suspected as a major factor in heart attack and stroke) and even reduce blood sugar. Not surprisingly, many physicians appreciate the comment that the only cause of death whose risk is not increased by obesity is suicide.

Currently a good deal of confusion about obesity exists. Not even its definition is precise, for while some doctors speak of it as being twenty pounds or more above the desirable weight for height and age (as shown in standard tables), others say the measure is 20 percent or more above the ideal figure. An important factor here is how much of one's weight is fat and how much actual muscle. Doctors can determine this today with a simple technique: by merely pinching or lifting a fold of skin over the triceps of the arm and measuring this skinfold with a special pair of calipers. From this figure and standard tables, doctors can quickly tell the amount of body fat and whether a patient is obese or just heavily muscled.

The factors involved in obesity are many and complex, and, generally, physicians are pessimistic about dealing with this problem. The reasons people are obese are not yet really understood—whether, for example, the problem is cultural, emotional, metabolic, or genetic; or, as seems likely, if it is due to a number of these factors whose relative importance varies with each person. However, obesity does result either from excessive intake of calories or from using up less of them. A fat person doesn't always consume more calories than a thin one.

Fat people, however, do often eat more food at one sitting, eat more rapidly, and eat when they're not hungry (at night, say, or under emotional stress). Childhood obesity may be initiated by the stress of a broken home, the death of a parent, or emotional illness. Nibbling also results in a greater increase of body fat than eating the same amount of calories in one meal. The way the body utilizes or burns its sugars also plays a major role in obesity. Malfunction of endocrine glands such as the pancreas, thyroid, and adrenals has also been associated with obesity in some people. Pregnancy or the pill may also produce obesity by increasing appetite and water retention.

One theory increasingly accepted today is that while infants are not born obese, the predisposition to obesity is established in infancy, perhaps between birth and five years of age. The obese child has a greater number of large fat cells (the cells are large because they are "stuffed" with a fat called triglyceride). Infants are born with a fifth to a quarter of the total number of the fat cells they will have as adults and with about a quarter of their adult total body fat content. A person's fat cells are formed under nutritional and hormonal control during the last weeks before birth, the first year of life, and in early adolescence.

Girls' fat cells are significantly larger than boys', and so infant girls are usually fatter. While the fat cell size normally does not increase significantly, the total number of these cells roughly quadruples between the ages of five and fifteen years and remains stable thereafter. As boys become leaner during their growth spurt and sexual maturation, their total body fat level declines (to 7.9 percent as compared with 22.8 percent for girls), but girls do continue to deposit tissue fat until sixteen or seventeen years of age, after which this tendency normally slackens off.

There seem to be two peaks of juvenile obesity—in the first year of life and in early to mid-adolescence. One study has shown that of one hundred overweight boys and girls, 80 percent of the overweight girls and 86 percent of the overweight boys became overweight adults.

Just how many adolescents are obese is really not known, but the usual figures are 9 percent of teen-age boys and 12.5 percent of girls. Parents should be careful, however, before becoming overly concerned about overweight youngsters—because the preadolescent and the teen-ager are likely to be plump just before the growth spurt. It's almost as if nature were preparing the youngster for a period of peak food need. It's unwise to cut calories without professional advice, because it's been shown that obese youngsters do not always take in more calories than the normal-weight ones. Obese, inactive girls actually take in fewer calories than their lean peers. Moreover, decreasing the caloric intake of overweight adolescents has been found, at times, to stunt the growth of these youngsters. Reducing body fat safely at this age is most difficult, because it can lead to loss of protein, which is harmful to growth. Teen-agers should not be put on severe diets if this can be at all avoided. They may, however, be taught to eat properly and, once excess weight is removed, taught not to regain it.

Safe Reducing

With such limited and changing knowledge of adolescent obesity, it is essential to work closely with your youngster's doctor in planning diet and activity schedules. For example, the plump boy or girl may go through a growth spurt and come out a slender teen-ager whose fat has all been moved around by nature to end up in the right and most attractive places. Parents should avoid fussing about weight until they have discussed it in detail with the youngster's physician. Many young people who feel that their parents want them to do one thing will simply do the opposite.

The handling of teen-age obesity should start with a medical consultation to decide whether overweight really *is* obesity, or whether it may not disappear by itself shortly. If it is a problem, then one must study how to motivate the youngster to do whatever is necessary. Very often the growth spurt, with its growing sexual maturation and heterosexual interest (usually accompanied by interest in one's own body), presents a golden opportunity to spark the youngster's interest in slimming down.

In most cases, success in treating the obese adolescent is difficult. A doctor's friendliness and concern are essential to insure the teen-ager's cooperation through the months or years needed to reach correct weight. Weekly counseling sessions may be necessary, along with incentives and rewards. Exercises are prescribed and increased; adequate supplemental vitamins along with proper daily amounts of protein, carbohydrates, and fat are planned. Amphetamine drugs, thyroid, or sex hormones are to be condemned. A recently introduced extract of urine from normal individuals may be of value, but is still only experimental and needs far more testing to find out why and how hormones in urine reduce body fat. Intestinal surgery (so-called bypass or jejunoileal shunt) has caused too many dangerous side effects and is too drastic. Psychological counseling or psychotherapy may be helpful in some, but it may also intensify the youngster's feelings of hopelessness, rejection, and anger if not handled properly.

The best approach to teen-age obesity is prevention: caloric intake should be regulated from infancy, especially during the first year of life and the preadolescent years (nine to eleven). Evidence indicates that infant obesity may be prevented by keeping the infant on breast milk or formula with no solids until the infant is at least six months of age.

PROPER NUTRITION

The nutritional needs of teen-agers are so great and so crucial that any dieting must be medically supervised. A doctor may even turn the youngster over to a special nutritional counselor for long-term help and followup. The fad diets today and the use of vitamins (usually unnecessary) are a very troublesome aspect of current teen-age nutrition. Studies have shown that family relationships and health attitudes are vital. When there is open communication with respect shown for the youngster's beliefs and questions, proper information can be conveyed.

Dr. Evelyn B. Spindler, Department of Agriculture nutritionist and an expert on teen-age food habits, has found that youngsters blame their own hurry and overactivity for their lack of proper eating, and put the responsibility for proper food habits and meals on their mothers. So there is a door open through which they can be reached—if you can find the way through it. Correcting family food habits as new scientific information becomes available is a good way to teach teen-agers that eating should be on both a rational and a good nutritional basis. Teen-age obesity and nutrition are one of the newest and least understood areas of medical knowledge, so work closely with your youngster's physician here.

Good nutrition requires an intake of protein daily of one gram per kilogram of body weight from age eleven to age fourteen and of nine-tenths of a gram per kilogram per day from age fifteen to age twenty-two. This applies to both sexes, as do the needs of forty-five milligrams of vitamin C and of 400 I.U. (international units) of vitamin D per day from age eleven to age twenty-two. A newly discovered essential mineral, zinc, is needed in about the same daily amounts (fifteen milligrams per day) for both sexes from age eleven to age twenty-two.

The daily requirement of vitamin A is 5,000 I.U. for boys at all ages, but girls need only 4,000 I.U. per day. The need for iron is eighteen milligrams per day in boys until the age of eighteen (after which age they need only ten milligrams per day). Girls need eighteen milligrams of iron from ages eleven to twenty-two. In both sexes, calcium must be supplied in the diet at 1,200 milligrams per day to maintain bone and dental metabolism.

Actually, the vast majority of teen-agers eat diets adequate for their growth and energy requirements— thanks to a combination of mobility, spending money, and the variety of foods they eat. Although any particular day's diet may be inadequate, they do average out to acceptable patterns, and dietary supplements of vitamins or of iron are rarely necessary. However, vitamin and iron deficiencies— anemias—are found in adolescents who have gone on fad diets.

ANEMIAS

Teen-age girls suffer iron-deficiency anemias roughly only half as often as boys—and the girls do so as a result of fad dieting or heavy menses. Boys become anemic because their rapid rate of growth in middle or late adolescence needs iron for both red blood cells and muscles. When the iron demand outstrips the dietary supply, anemia results. This is shown by a single simple blood test for hemoglobin (more complex and sensitive blood studies are sometimes needed). Treatment takes the form of oral iron tablets for several months.

Sickle-cell anemia (seen in only one in 1,000 American blacks) may not even be diagnosed until a doctor notes growth retardation, delayed sexual maturation, or regular anemia that doesn't respond to iron tablets. Boys suffer sexual maturation delays more often than girls, who may have difficulty conceiving or carrying to term. Young people afflicted with sickle-cell anemia suffer feelings of peer rejection, fear of future vocational limitations, and of social life failures—and psychological counseling is often necessary.

Sickle-cell anemia is a genetic (autosomal recessive) disease in which hemoglobin (the essential protein in red blood cells) is chemically defective, resulting in the red blood cell's inability to carry oxygen. The defective blood cells themselves have an abnormal sickle shape. Dizziness and shortness of breath are signs of the disease, which is generally not fatal, although there is no cure for it yet.

The mere presence of the sickle-cell trait has caused undue alarm and anxiety, for the only time such people suffer symptoms is at high altitudes, under general anesthesia, or in deep-sea diving.

ANOREXIA NERVOSA

Anorexia nervosa is one of the more bizarre and frightening problems of adolescence, because it leaves its victims looking like concentration-camp inmates, and it is sometimes fatal. Ironically, it strikes mainly the adolescent daughters of the affluent, educated, and successful; and the condition has been increasing rapidly in the last fifteen years. It was first described a little over a century ago when it was given its name—which literally means nervous or emotional loss of appetite. The Germans call it *Magersucht* or "a mania to be thin," and that's what it is—self-inflicted starvation. Although it occurs in prepuberty or very early adulthood (before the age of twenty-five), it is typically a problem of adolescent girls, who suffer it ten times as often as boys do.

Dr. Hilde Bruch, Baylor College of Medicine professor of psychiatry and leading authority on this disorder, has only seen about ninety cases in thirty years. She points out a study that has recently revealed that roughly one girl in 200 in English private schools suffered the condition, although only one in 3,000 was affected in the public schools. The disease is international and has been reported widely in Europe and in Australia. The condition is primarily a psychiatric disturbance. Dr. Bruch believes it arises from conflicts within the family and from fear of sexuality. Most young victims appear to conform to their parents' wishes without expressing or following their own. Their refusal to eat is their only defiance. The youngster usually feels increasingly isolated and helpless, but by not eating and refusing to be made to do so, she feels (on an unconscious level) that she is finally assuming control of herself and her body. Parental pressure and anger only drive the young girl into a greater demonstration and use of what appears to this child as a power previously unknown to her, starvation.

Girls suffering from anorexia lose tremendous amounts of weight rapidly—so that they may fall from one hundred twenty pounds to under eighty within a couple of months. Their weight losses can run 40 percent and more, and their menstrual periods cease. Parents become increasingly alarmed and impotent. Although anorexic girls say they feel "full" after a few bites of food, many show a preoccupation with food and eat minuscule amounts often and very slowly over long periods. Sometimes when they eat a reasonable amount of food they will make themselves vomit or take enemas or laxatives regularly. They may also show bursts of overactivity without the fatigue you would expect in a malnourished child. Despite eating little, they always deny feeling hungry.

Therapy must consist of a two-pronged attack—first is the medical treatment for malnutrition and starvation; and second is the simultaneous psychiatric treatment of the underlying emotional problems. It's not an easy task, and even the best efforts may end in failure, leaving the young people to suffer with their problem and perhaps to die from the starvation or the malnourished's susceptibility to disease. Fewer than half of patients recover from A. N.

Most youngsters must be hospitalized to correct their malnutrition. Some physicians resort to tube-feeding, but this should be done only with those too weak to take food by mouth. Concerned supportive medical care with an establishment of personal rapport between doctor and youngster will help. But the medical personnel must never coerce, criticize, or punish these unfortunate adolescents; they must always treat them as suffering human beings who need help desperately.

Discharge from the hospital should be followed by regular visits for a considerable time to her doctor. A month or more in the hospital and several months of close medical supervision, accompanied by long-term observation and psychotherapy, is called for until the youngster has come to grips with her problem and no longer feels the need to starve herself. Family therapy is often effective. It's a long haul for youngster, family, and doctor—but if it's successful it will provide a normal healthy future for the suffering adolescent.

Twelve

PROBLEMS OF
SEXUAL MATURATION

I N many ways the greatest change during the teens, and the most significant, certainly the most highly charged emotionally, is sexual maturation. For the girl, a tremendously dramatic and abrupt change leads her into a new way of life, and a number of problems may accompany this transition. The boys, too, are likely to suffer disturbing problems. The sudden outpouring of sex hormones carries boys and girls alike into a new physical world as they travel through their teens.

ACNE

Most teen-agers spend inordinate amounts of time in front of a mirror as they observe, minutely and critically, their face and skin and body. At puberty the flawlessly smooth skin of the very young suddenly turns into something quite different as acne, the terrible bane of adolescence, makes its appearance. A survey of almost a half century ago revealed that over 90 percent of teen-aged boys and 80 percent of adolescent girls suffer from the condition technically called *acne vulgaris* or common acne.

Acne is the most common skin disease of the teen years. So common is it in fact that some dermatologists feel it might almost be considered physiological or functional, rather than pathological or diseased. But to the teen-ager it is the supreme tragedy, because it sets him apart, further damaging his weak ego. Each new pimple becomes a major catastrophe. Medicine can today offer much help to the acne patient.

Acne is a ten-year scourge whose presence the teen-ager cannot deny (as he can do with diseases like diabetes, where the problem is buried inside his body and no one can see). Acne is right out there where neither he nor his peers can ignore it—and it seems to have a habit of kicking up every time he has something important lined up (a big date or important affair). At such times even one big red pimple is enough to devastate and destroy the young person who is trying so hard to show his best face.

Dr. Marion B. Sulzberger, dermatologist and professor emeritus at New York University, says that acne is the source of more family difficulties and fights than almost any other disorder. While many parents blame the youngster ("You don't get enough sleep" . . . "You eat too much" . . . "You think of sex all the time"), the teen-ager is often angry and resentful of the smooth skin of his or her parents.

Because of acne's visibility, frequency, and long dura-tion, there are probably more myths woven about its cause than about any other skin problem. Acne really has nothing to do with sexual frustration or activity, nor does it reveal when a girl is menstruating, nor is it inherited or due to dirt or to bad eating habits. It is, in fact, a complex disease that is not yet fully understood, but help is nevertheless available.

Actually it all starts with the adolescent's increased production of male sex hormone, testosterone. Both boys and girls have this hormone, although girls have far less of it. Enough is produced by the adrenal glands, even in girls, to cause enlargement of the sebaceous or oil glands that lie deep in the skin, where they have been ever since birth. These glands pour oils or sebum into a series of tiny tubes (the follicular canals), which contain minute hairs and whose openings on the skin are the pores. Acne may be found on the face, neck, back, and chest. On the forehead, for example, there are an estimated 2,000 sebaceous glands per square inch.

As the sebaceous glands enlarge under the influence of testosterone, they also produce more sebum and keratin (the fibrous, tough protein or horny substance on the surface of all skin). Ordinarily the cells lining the follicle are sloughed off regularly to be carried by the oil up to the pores and discharged. But in the teen-ager with acne, these dead cells clump together in the follicles and, with too much keratin, act to plug up the skin pores. Bacteria deep in the follicles secrete enzymes that convert the oil to fatty acids that irritate the skin tissues.

This plug of sebum, bacteria, keratin, and dead cells is called a *comedo* (*comedones* is the plural). When a comedo pushes through a pore to reach the skin surface it turns dark, a "blackhead." When the comedo remains within the follicle it's a "whitehead" and forms a small grainlike mass, which may rupture into the surrounding skin tissues and produce inflamed lumps (papules, pustules, nodules) under the skin.

These lumps in turn may lead to pus formation (pustules) and eventually acne cysts may result. These cysts are deeply buried inflammatory conditions that may remain for months, spilling some of their contents onto the skin surface every so often. When acne is severe and full-blown, these pus-filled lesions appear as yellowish pustules surrounded by red inflamed tissues, the typical large, angry red pimples one sees in a bad acne condition. Fortunately most acne does not go on to this level but stops at an earlier stage and remains a relatively mild condition.

Treatment varies with the severity of the condition, but care should begin as soon as the condition is noticeable. A visit to the teen-ager's regular doctor should be made as soon as the acne is visible. The doctor may suggest some mild home care—hygienic measures and perhaps some over-the-counter medications. When the acne is severe, he will probably recommend a dermatologist.

This specialist will remove some of the comedones with special instruments, and prescribe medications newly available. One of the most useful of the drugs is vitamin A acid, tretinoin, but there are other locally applied materials that may also be used. These may produce various reactions, but under skilled care acne scarring can be kept to a minimum and the condition itself controlled. Sometimes, too, antibiotics may be prescribed.

The psychological effects of acne vary with the teenager. It's important that somebody cares about the problem and that it's not just passed off as another thing the teenager has to learn to live with.

MENARCHE AND MENSTRUAL PROBLEMS

It is in her gynecological difficulties that the adolescent girl chiefly differs, so far as medical problems are concerned, from the adult woman. In this area, the teen-ager's disorders are essentially those concerned with the development and maturation of her menstrual functions—menarche and the new patterns of the menstrual process, the developing cycle with its erratic early nature, its emotional impact, its meaning, and its pain. In some ways the emotional problems are more prominent, more dominant, and more important than the physical ones.

The menarche itself is a major watershed in an adolescent girl's life—psychologically, sexually, and physically. On one side stands childhood and on the other womanhood—and the transition is dramatic and seemingly abrupt. As one mother expressed her emotions about her daughter, who had menstruated for the first time while on a trip away from home: "I saw a child get onto the plane and a woman came back just a few weeks later." Menstruation is a landmark of tremendous significance, far more spectacular and significant than any of the other changes that precede and herald the coming menarche—the appearance and growth of the breast buds and the pubic hair, the alterations in figure and hips. All these other changes pale before the suddenness of the first menstruation. The enormous psychological impact of this dramatic occurrence makes it easy to understand why extensive mythology and folk beliefs have grown up around both menarche and menstrual periods.

A young girl feels this vast change acutely, both before and after the menarche, so it is not surprising that this event has the capacity to trigger a great amount of psychological turmoil. Some young girls eagerly await their first period, which will permit them to "join the club." They feel left out as they see and hear older sisters or friends gather to discuss hygienic measures or tampons and talk of situations that have arisen and how to handle boys. To this teen-age girl, her first menstruation is the ultimate proof of her own growth and femininity, the long-awaited "now I am a woman."

On the other hand, there is the young girl whose closest ties have been to the father rather than to the mother, whose desire for identification has been with the male parent. This is the tomboy who ran with the boys and not the girls, and to such youngsters menstruation can actually bring a feeling of disaster. Menstruation moves her finally and irretrievably into an alien female world. In addition, if her first menstrual period is a painful one (and with her negative feelings about it, it's more than likely to be traumatic), then the menstrual period becomes what it has so long been called—"the curse," or "the sickness."

Menarche can be either a gratifying and fulfilling experience, or an inconvenience. With a personality and self-image still unformed and immature, it is certainly not surprising to find a frightened girl who confuses reality with myth and poorly understood facts with superstition.

The best way to avoid emotional trauma, or at least to keep it to a minimum, is to prepare your daughter for this crucial life experience. Arm her with the knowledge of the changes she will experience, the causes, and the meaning. If you have chosen the right doctor, he or she will be sensitive to all the problems and can help your daughter understand the process.

Long before adolescence, a physician will probably have done some kind of examination of the genitals (boys are always examined, but doctors in the past have hesitated to examine young girls). Such procedures provide the opportunity to acquaint the youngster with the anatomy and functioning of the reproductive system. In fact, most practitioners examine the female genitalia externally from infancy and occasionally see young girls as early as three years of age for discharges and urination problems. Checking anatomical development and checking for infection should be part of the annual exam. Thus, doctors can help prepare young girls for menarche and menstruation in a realistic and factual way. Doctors are also a source for a girl to seek information and to discuss sexual life and contraceptive needs without having to approach her parents (which many teen-agers are hesitant to do) and without having to rely on information gleaned from her peers.

Doctors who treat many adolescents find that it's commonly the mothers and not the daughters who are concerned with a late menarche. Even though the onset of menstruation in the United States today can be anywhere from nine to seventeen years of age, the teen-ager herself is likely to become concerned if by the age of fifteen she still hasn't menstruated. When gynecological problems arise in teen-agers, it's best to have the girls see their regular doctor first before they see a specialist. Young girls will feel more comfortable with the family physician, who can prepare them for what to expect at the gynecologist's office. The referral of an adolescent to a specialist creates a good deal of anxiety in the teen-ager—and many if not most gynecologists are likely to treat her as they are accustomed to treat adult women. The typical gynecologist simply walks in and goes to work without preliminaries or ceremony. Your youngster's physician should, whenever possible, refer her to a specialist (if one is needed) who treats a lot of teen-agers and can relate well to them. If such specialized care is needed and a doctor skilled in handling teen-agers can't be found, the youngster's physician can prepare her for this experience of dealing with a specialist. He can explain what will be done and why, how the specialist will act and what the visit will be like so that though it may be an unpleasant experience for the young woman, it will at least not be a traumatic one.

Actually, such specialized care is rarely necessary, because adolescent physicians can usually handle 80 or 90 percent or more of the problems that teen-agers bring to their offices. But if there has been no menstruation by the age of seventeen, or if more than five years have passed since the beginning of breast development, parent and teen-ager have reason to question the situation. There may be many reasons for this lack of menstruation (amenorrhea), including emotional problems, endocrine difficulties, or even pathology (disease). Today, doctors have many different ways to test and treat this problem. They may try hormones to induce menstruation (five days of such treatment and the periods often start within a week), or refer the young woman to experts for specialized examinations and tests to locate and diagnose the trouble. Amenorrhea can be due to a failure of the ovaries to develop, a genetic abnormality called "Turner's syndrome." However, physical examination may reveal other less common causes, such as a small or absent uterus, or simply an imperforate hymen (one with no opening). Such a hymen may even be bulging with backed-up menstrual blood and is readily correctible by very simple surgery.

It's been said, however, that girls must "practice" menstruating before they can achieve their regular cycle, and it may take as many as forty-eight menstrual periods before the regular cycle and the adult-type menstrual periods take over. The age at which menarche occurs has no influence on this initial irregularity, and early cycles can span anywhere from three to six weeks. Discomfort or pain just before the period, or during its first day or two, is common among teen-agers, and it will usually increase as they move along into the later years of adolescence.

The causes of menstrual pain are still a matter of considerable conjecture. When no physical cause can be found for the pain, it is assumed to be psychological, such as the emotional expression of the fear of bleeding or of feelings about being a woman; or a whole host of erroneous beliefs may be involved. Where one girl will complain of severe pain, another may totally ignore the discomfort and not be bothered by it.

No better evidence is given of the way emotions as well as stress are involved in menstruation than some observations of Dr. Katharina Dalton, noted British physician and menstrual cycle expert: she relates that when groups of schoolgirls are taken abroad, one of the problems that arises is the unexpectedly large numbers of girls who menstruate. Many have their menarche on such occasions. In one girl's boarding school where ninety-one girls between the ages of fourteen and seventeen were undergoing examinations that would vitally influence their future careers, almost exactly half suffered altered menstrual cycles. In many, these cycles were lengthened; in some, shortened; and some skipped their periods entirely. Where in a normal day sixteen girls on the average could have been expected to menstruate, during these examinations as many as thirty-six did.

Any abnormal menstrual situation calls for a medical consultation, because things can go wrong physically with the teen-ager as with the adult. For teen-agers to miss a period or two is quite common—except that today the first thing doctor and parents think of in any teen-ager, no matter how young, is pregnancy. Only after doctors have checked for this do they begin to wonder whether the lapse is the perfectly normal irregularity of the teen years or some other disturbance.

Dysmenorrhea—painful menstruation—is common in middle and late adolescence. The condition can vary from the very mild to the incapacitating—the more severe forms seem to occur in sedentary youngsters rather than in athletic ones, and in those with chronic illnesses. Dysmenorrhea may consist of mild abdominal cramps or nausea or even vomiting for one or two days before the menses, and it is often relieved by a heavy initial flow. Less common among adolescents is the congestive type of dysmenorrhea, with a "water-logged" feeling of the head or back, tenderness and tightness of the breasts, and fatigue and irritability for several days before the menstrual period.

Reassurance, a heating pad, and simple painkillers are sufficient for mild problems. For more severe ones, sex hormones will prevent ovulation and relieve symptoms for several months. Once the youngster is taken off the medication, she will establish her own cycle naturally by herself. Occasionally, however, for really troublesome dysmenorrhea, young girls may even need psychotherapy.

MALE BREAST ENLARGEMENT

A fourteen-year-old boy was cutting his physical education classes and avoiding going to the beach with his gang. He was clearly worried. After being gently questioned, he finally admitted to his father that he was developing breasts. Ashamed and fearful of turning feminine, he was hiding. Medical examinations soon reassured the boy that in another year or two nature would resolve the whole problem.

Actually a large number of adolescent boys—some experts say as many as half—have a noticeable growth of breast tissue in the early years of puberty. While some boys have only a "breast button" (a small, tender enlargement beneath and around the areola), others have an enlargement of one or both breasts that may look distinctly feminine and that occasionally even reaches the size of the fully mature female breast. When the change is limited to the breast button, it is termed adolescent gynecomastia or, more technically, benign adolescent hypertrophy of the breast. These buttons are commonly discovered only when the teen-ager washes the area.

Male breast enlargements are thought to be due to the imbalance of male and female sex hormones at puberty. The majority of young boys develop these breast conditions about the time the penis and scrotum enlarge and the pubic hair increases. These breast enlargements persist for a year or two and then disappear by themselves. Reassurance is all that is necessary. Only very rarely (in perhaps 1 percent of such problems) is there any genetic or endocrine abnormality, and for these rarities, hormone therapy (after extensive examination) may be instituted.

Sometimes, however, so much emotional disturbance results that it becomes virtually incapacitating. Doctors may then feel that, particularly where the breast enlargement is very marked, the psychological health of the adolescent necessitates cosmetic surgery. In such relatively rare and extreme instances, careful surgery (a mastectomy, in fact) by an expert in the field may be advised to remove excess breast tissue, leaving only a tiny scar below nipple and areola.

It is essential that boys with any breast enlargements see a doctor, for sometimes hormonal problems or even tumors have caused gynecomastia, but this is truly rare and doctors don't even consider it before a thorough examination. Treatment, depending on what the doctor finds, will be aimed at eliminating the condition's cause.

THE TESTICLES

Normally the testes or testicles develop in the fetus and migrate from the abdomen down into the scrotum less than two months before birth. Testes that don't reach the scrotum but stay within the abdomen or inguinal canal (the pathway from abdomen to scrotum) may become sterile (probably due to the higher temperature within the abdomen). Cryptorchidism (an undescended testicle) must be differentiated by the doctor from the very common mobile testicle, which can be nursed down into the scrotum with special manipulation. Such testes, which can be brought down when there is no hernia present, are perfectly normal. These youngsters have what is called an active cremasteric reflex, a condition in which the testes are retracted into the inguinal canal when the boy is cold or embarrassed or otherwise psychologically disturbed.

However, when the testicles are truly undescended, surgical correction may be needed. The operation (called orchiopexy) to bring down and fix the testes in the scrotum is performed to protect against injury to the testicle in the inguinal canal and to avoid the increased risk of cancerous change (both in the undescended testis as well as its mate, which may have descended). Only when both testes are undescended will the boy almost invariably be sterile. The age for such surgery has varied until recently from about three to the early teens. Large studies have now shown that the operation should be performed early because no cancers developed in testes brought down before six years of age. The use of hormones to cause testicles to descend is no longer considered worthwhile and should be avoided.

Another problem here is nontraumatic pain (pain not due to an injury or blow). One of the two most common causes of such pain is torsion of the testicle, in which an abnormal rotation of the testis reduces or cuts off its blood supply. The testicle and scrotum become painful, dark, and swollen, and the youngster often suffers nausea, vomiting, or abdominal pain, which usually come on very suddenly and may even appear after intensive activity or following an injury during a game. The only treatment here is immediate surgery to restore the blood circulation to normal, so as to preserve the health of this vital organ.

In adolescents, however, the other most common cause of nontraumatic testicular pain comes on more gradually. This is a condition called torsion of the appendix testis. This problem is due to a twisting of the testicle at its upper end, where there is a tiny nubbin of tissue left over from fetal life. This too causes intense pain, swelling, stomachache, and a variety of other such symptoms. Immediate and temporary treatment consists of bed rest, elevation of the scrotum with a suspensory, and mild painkillers. Final resolution of the problem is accomplished with surgery for the removal of this tiny bit of tissue at the upper end of the testis, which is untouched in the operation.

Sometimes there is a condition called varicocele, a condition of elongated and tortuous scrotal veins (essentially varicose veins of the scrotum). These can cause a heavy or dragging sensation in the groin, scrotum, or lower abdomen. Most of these varicosities subside when the youngster lies down, and they can be treated simply by having the boy wear jockey shorts. Only rarely is there so much severe and persistent discomfort that surgery is necessary to correct the problem. Surgery has also been done for extremely large varicoceles, which appear to be prone to increased sterility.

Thirteen

TROUBLED—OR TROUBLESOME—TEEN-AGER?

ADOLESCENTS are troublesome to you the parents, but even more so to themselves. At least parents have enough knowledge and experience to be able to view turbulent and confused teen-agers with detachment and understanding, to be able to enjoy the stimulating, challenging, and exciting period of growth. But teen-agers themselves have little experience and cannot view themselves with any objectivity—nor are they aware that their behavior and actions *are* bizarre or irrational, or that their wide swings of moods, attitudes, and interests are anything but ordinary human traits.

Many parents may find that they have to solve a difficult problem that can even stump the experts: parents are the first to decide when and if the very troublesome teen-ager has turned into the troubled one, if the "normal" teen-ager has become the abnormal or emotionally ill adolescent. To find your way through all the conflict and turmoil of this period and reach a calm, rational judgment, you need help. Here are the red flags, the warning signals, *you* should look out for to determine if psychiatric care is warranted.

WHAT IS A NORMAL ADOLESCENT?

Many adolescents ambivalently swing from extreme to extreme; they are adult and child simultaneously, independent and dependent (and insist on being treated in both ways). Emotional growth and development are erratic, unpredictable, and highly individual—no one can predict the precise patterns of individual progression.

One father said of his household with its two teen-agers: "This place reminds me of the old-time movies, the *Perils of Pauline*—those weekly movie serials with their recurring crises and their last-second respites and reprieves, the waiting with bated breath for the next explosion." A mother wondered about her teen-agers: "If this is normal—tell me what in God's name is *abnormal?*" And a physician on the staff of a leading East Coast psychiatric hospital remarked, "If teen-agers were judged by adult standards they would all have to be considered psychotic."

There is virtually only one thing on which everyone agrees: a perfectly smooth developmental pattern without any emotional upheavals, conflict, or turbulence in an adolescent *is* cause for concern, *is* abnormal! All too often such total calm may in fact indicate that the youngster is repressing his or her problems and failing to work through the necessary changes of this phase of life. Very frequently, such a calm teen-ager will pay a dear price for skipping the essential task of maturation and suffer with unresolved serious personality disturbances later on in his or her adult life.

What helps to confuse the picture is that the "normal" process of adolescence varies so widely both in its manifestations and its time frame that it is more practical to look at the ways and signs doctors use to indicate the adolescents who are in need of professional help. With the news media filled with reports of teen-agers' transgressions—the delinquency and the dropouts, the violence and the drug addiction, the runaways and the suicides—it takes an expert to bring a breath of cold, hard realism into the picture. For in spite of all the dramatic popular stories that parents may read, most of today's adolescents actually do function competently in most areas of their daily lives a great part of the time.

RECOGNIZING THE DISTURBED TEEN-AGER

What is surprising is not that there are so many emotionally ill adolescents, but that there are so few. Figures indicate that adolescent psychiatric or psychological help is asked for by 20 percent of the teen-agers when it is made available. It's been said too that 10 percent of the illnesses that college students suffer are actually psychosomatic, emotional in their origin, and one survey found that some three-quarters of the students who felt they needed help were despondent or depressed.

Fortunately, psychological help from a wide range of

professionals is readily available to disturbed teen-agers today, and the success obtained is considerable. Certainly there is no better proof of the increase in the numbers of emotionally ill young people than to look at the startling growth in their suicide and accident rates (many observers believe that most accidents are to a large extent hidden suicides). Suicide, however, is so important an issue that we will save it for our next chapter.

The techniques used to identify the disturbed adolescent vary, but young people generally show their problems in the form of anxiety, tension, restlessness, sleep disturbances, and such psychosomatic disorders as headaches, asthma, menstrual disturbances, and intestinal problems. Troubled teen-agers also commonly test those whose good opinions they want and value by behaving in unreasonable and outrageous ways. The disturbed adolescent, for example, will not be susceptible to reasoning, while the normal teen-ager can be reasoned with most of the time. The emotionally ill teen-ager will also act in a self-defeating fashion not just for the moment (as normal youngsters do) but over the long run, and his actions will make no sense either to himself or to others for a very considerable period of time. Nor can he be reached by those who should be closest to him under normal circumstances. Delinquency is another sign of the emotionally ill child, as is acting-out behavior such as stealing, suicidal attempts, or repeated accidents, drug abuse, and sexual promiscuity.

Doctors also find that disturbed youngsters commonly have a variety of symptoms. Physicians quickly recognize certain physical or emotional complaints such as tension or restlessness as symptoms of anxiety. Teen-agers may suffer psychosomatic disorders as well. Only a minority of adolescents actually need psychiatric treatment; however, determining which ones do need such care calls for a subtle understanding of the differences between adolescent turmoil and serious emotional disturbances. Two key indicators are, first, the complaint of any teen-ager that he has such a problem; and, second, the concern of the family about its teen-ager's adjustment problems. Both such situations must be taken very seriously, and given full consideration.

Dr. Mark J. Blotcky, of the Department of Child and Adolescent Psychiatry at Dallas's Timberlawn Hospital, suggests to physicians certain guidelines to follow in deciding whether a particular young patient needs psychiatric help. Parents can follow this advice too.

1.) Determine the teen-ager's general mood and how he himself thinks he's doing; try to determine what the teenager thinks of himself.

2.) Watch how the teen-ager functions in the family, because this is particularly helpful in understanding his strengths, his needs, and his character style. Note how he gets along with the other members of the family and how they get along with each other. It's important to recognize any underlying family disturbances, problems, or stresses, such as whether arguments linger on either as smoldering fire or as silent grudges (one fourteen year old complained that when her mother was angry she wouldn't say anything for days).

3.) Examine the teen-ager's relations with friends and peers—the normal teen-ager can make solid friendships. See whether he has friends or is lonely and shy; whether the relationships are transitory or stable and supportive. By middle adolescence, an interest in the opposite sex should begin. It's often helpful to ask a youngster to describe his best friend, because the normal adolescent can provide an alive, in-depth personality profile of his friend, where he is likable and where not. The disturbed teen-ager will often draw a monotonous, flat picture with only a single characteristic included.

4.) Evaluate the adolescent's school performance. Here one can learn how well the teen-ager gets along with authorities outside the family. Find out whether teachers like him; whether there is any truancy or withdrawal; what interest there is in extracurricular activities. The relationship between his grades and intelligence, as well as what his family expects of him, may also help to reveal problem areas, such as anxieties and inhibitions, poor toleration of frustration, inadequate impulse control (one sixteen-year-old boy immediately threw anything he held in his hand when he became angry), depression, or even the energies he is using up in other emotional conflicts.

5.) Consider extracurricular activities. The normal teen-ager pours time and energy (after school or on weekends or holidays) into numerous productive and pleasurable activities with friends, such as athletics or hobbies, or various volunteer organizations. Prolonged, bored idleness may indicate problems.

6.) Watch for the pathological (sickness-indicating) patterns—antisocial, self-destructive, and far-out behavior such as breaking the law, destroying property, attacking people, drug abuse, sexual promiscuity, the misuse of birth control techniques (becoming pregnant is often a form of acting-out, as we explored in Chapter 5). Does the youngster look unkempt or speak roughly? Has he ever run away?

Of course, such obvious problems as hallucinations (hearing voices, for example) or paranoid complaints ("the teachers are all out to get me") or other strange and divorced-from-reality ideas call for prompt consultation with a psychiatrist or a physician. Mood variations—frequent or persistent upsets like crying jags, depression, insomnia, loss of appetite—also warrant a visit to a doctor.

Measuring your own adolescent by such general tests will reassure you in most cases, since the majority of adolescents are normal and do function effectively and well in most areas most of the time. Of course you must judge young people as teen-agers and accept that they will behave in ways that do seem odd by adult standards.

The price that untreated teen-age emotional disturbance exacts can be tragically high and take its toll over many years, even through the youngster's subsequent entire adult life. Take the fifteen-year-old Midwestern boy who wrote his brother (away at college) long despairing letters. A brilliant teen-ager, a "good boy" in the sense that he did what his parents wanted, the letters were his only possible cry for help. The parents were immigrants and dictatorial, bent on forcing the boy into conformity with their judgments based on limited education and knowledge. Giving in to their wishes, he became an accountant and even chose behavior, friends, clothes, and life-style to satisfy them.

Seriously ill with psychosomatic disorders, he covered up with surface obedience a volcano of teen-age rage and rebellion, a seething caldron of explosive feelings that found a safety outlet in illnesses. Not until a middle-aged identity crisis and long-term psychotherapy finally freed him did he become the successful artist he had always really wanted to be—and he only then worked out his adolescent problems. Psychiatrists all tell of many similar tragically damaged patients.

Disturbed behavior in their children is often the most difficult thing for parents to recognize and admit (even to themselves). Yet to do so may well save a youngster from a totally destroyed life by bringing him to trained professionals for help while there is still time.

GETTING HELP

One of the people most likely to recognize how much help your teen-ager may need is the adolescent physician. In fact, a disturbed teen-ager may be started on the road to emotional health by an interested physician. The physical examination gives the skilled physician familiar with adolescent problems the opportunity to get to know the teenager and to eliminate the possibility of any underlying medical disorders. A good doctor-patient relationship with the teen-ager makes it easier for the physician to refer the young patient for proper specialized help.

The competent adolescent physician is qualified to decide whether there is need for psychiatric help. The need for help is often first suggested by school authorities or teachers who may consult a school guidance counselor, school psychologist, or psychiatrist and ask them to approach the parents. The unhappy parents are likely at this point to turn for help and confirmation to their family doctor. However, parents may also of course be concerned on their own about their youngster and seek professional advice.

The proper doctor at this point should be warm and interested, concerned with the teen-ager, whom he regards and treats as a responsible individual. Once a proper relationship has been established, the doctor can be open and honest. He must not be officious or authoritarian or overbearing (any teen-ager will rebel against this), and he must show he knows what he is doing, is aware of his own competence, is a doctor to whom respect is due (as he shows respect to his young patient), and is positive about his advice and what should be done. If he advises psychiatric treatment, teen-agers will usually react defensively, saying, "I'm not crazy," or giving some other reason for not seeking help. This negativism requires careful handling, and mutual trust.

If the problem is of recent occurrence—such as a family move, or even a divorce or loss of a parent—the teen-ager's physician may well be able to deal with the matter himself, or he may suggest a specially trained psychologist, clergyman, or psychiatric social worker. But if the problem is very serious or of long standing, requiring more than a half-dozen visits, or representing a threat to the young person's whole future, then a psychiatrist who specializes in adolescents is needed.

The physician might well join his young patient for the first ten minutes of the initial visit with the psychiatrist. It might also be helpful for the youngster to continue seeing "his doctor" for some time concurrently with the psychiatric visits until it is sure that the adolescent will continue with his psychotherapy. In fact, immediate referrals to a psychiatrist or a psychiatric clinic may not always be possible, and the physician may have to support his young patient and work with him for a period while awaiting the first psychiatric visit.

Adolescent psychotherapy is a complex affair. The parents too must be involved in a variety of ways—sometimes to the extent of undergoing therapy themselves. This can help the parents themselves to grow and to resolve their own problems, and they may well welcome this opportunity to regain good relations.

RECOVERY

Although most adolescent emotional disorders are characterized by unpredictability and extreme variability, there is a heartening response to prompt and proper treatment. Teen-agers usually become emotionally ill only when they are deeply disturbed about something that is highly important to them; most often this involves their relationships with their parents, and only secondarily those with the opposite sex. Any problems are usually much less severe and hence much easier to resolve when the basic parental relationships have been warm and satisfying.

The outlook seems better if the symptoms come on very suddenly and are set off by a known external stress (parental death or divorce, severe illness, and the like). The outlook is also improved if it's possible to change the environment in which the teen-ager lives—the family structure, undesirable people with whom the teen-ager associates, living conditions, or stresses. Another factor that can improve the prognosis is the teen-ager's own feeling that he is loved by someone important to him (parent, relative, other adult, or friend).

Probably the most common problem is depression. Dr. Gisela Konopka, in fact, tells of a very recent study of 5,600 high school students, which revealed that the incidence of depression was second only to the common cold, sore throats, and coughs. This finding might explain the high rate of suicide among teen-agers, the subject of our next chapter.

Fourteen

TEEN-AGE SUICIDE: THE NEW EPIDEMIC

EVERY year nearly a half-million teen-agers try to commit suicide, and some 5,000 actually succeed. Moreover, many deaths reported as "accidental" are believed to be suicides. We are clearly in the midst of a wave of teen-age suicide epidemic in proportion, with the rate nearly tripling over the last twenty years. In fact, suicide today is the third leading cause of death in the fifteen- to nineteen-year-old group, exceeded only by accidents and cancer. And suicide has already reached second rank as a cause of death on our college campuses (exceeded only by accidents).

It is important for parents to know why teen-agers want to commit suicide, which teen-agers are in particular danger of carrying out their suicidal wish, what cues and clues they give beforehand, and even what the final warning signals are and where help is obtainable. Armed with this knowledge, you may be able to prevent such a tragedy. Finally, it is important to know how you can protect yourself should this tragedy strike your home as it does so many these days.

THE HISTORY AND THE TABOO

No society has been known to be entirely free of suicide. It was known in India some five or six thousand years ago, and it is recorded in the Old Testament as well.

Western attitudes toward suicide have varied. The ancient Greeks and Romans at different times fluctuated from condemnation, regarding suicide as a crime against the state, to admiration of it as a noble act of honor. During the Middle Ages the Christian Church condemned suicide as a form of murder inspired by the devil. Catholics still consider it a mortal sin. Americans today regard suicide as a disgrace.

When the idea of suicide prevention centers was introduced in 1950 it was generally hailed as an exciting and promising new approach. The NIMH provided governmental involvement and backing. Actually, though, governmental suicide prevention measures go back several thousand years. Plutarch tells of a sudden epidemic of suicide twenty-five hundred years ago among the young women of the Greek city Miletus that was stopped only by the threat of official shaming of the body by dragging it through the marketplace.

Much of our societal attitude toward suicide is still irrational and seems to arise out of that general taboo that surrounds death itself. It is the stigma attached to suicide that prompts physicians and families alike to hush up the cause of a suicide's death. The stigma is reflected in the clauses in life insurance policies penalizing suicides and the refusal of many religions to accord the usual burial rites.

Suicide's taboo in our culture has made it difficult for doctors to question patients about whether they are thinking of suicide or whether they have ever attempted it. This reluctance deprives doctors of the vital information needed to protect suicidal patients, and it deprives the patients themselves of the opportunity to ventilate their feelings and to gain expert advice. It is this taboo, in fact, that has often led public and medical professionals to characterize the suicide as mentally ill or psychotic, or to regard suicide as evidence of weakness and lack of courage. But suicide is a complex issue, and its causes are seldom simple to determine.

THE KINDS OF SUICIDE

It's best to understand the meaning of the suicide terms used here. *Completed suicide* means the taking of action that actually ends one's life. On the other hand, *suicide attempts* are meant to destroy the individual or to give the appearance of intending to do so. And *suicide ideas* are characteristic of people who indicate potential suicide attempts by obtaining the necessary lethal drugs or by talking of suicide. However, in such cases, the actual suicide is seldom carried out.

Almost nine out of ten suicide attempts take place in the teen-ager's own home, so that parents should not relax, thinking their children are "safe at home." Most at-home suicides use an overdose of some drug found in the house— barbiturates in about a third of the overdoses—and aspirin. As many as a quarter of all suicide attempters are actually repeaters—so those who have once attempted suicide are at a greater risk of succeeding the next time. Expert professional help should always be promptly sought the first time a teen-ager takes this very serious step. The suicide rate of previous attempters has been found to be more than sixty times as high as that in the population at large—and about half of the people who complete suicides have attempted it before.

Completed suicide obviously can never be treated—it can only be prevented. To learn about the impulses behind suicide, the experts in the field can only interview and analyze the people who have attempted suicide and failed. Insight may be cold comfort for the family of a completed suicide, but it may help someone who suffers repetitive suicide ideas.

WHY TEEN-AGERS COMMIT SUICIDE

Nobody really knows why anybody commits suicide. The teen-ager is particularly susceptible to depression, and this condition is a high-risk factor in suicides. To make matters worse, the use of alcohol aggravates the depression that plagues teen-agers because it is a depressant. If your teen-ager is depressed you should try to keep him from drinking—something admittedly easier said than done. A frank discussion may help alleviate the problem.

Recent studies indicate that feelings of hopelessness may be more involved with suicide than depression is. The adolescent struggling to cope with a rapidly changing world as well as with his own inner confusions and uncertainties, striving to become independent and yet afraid to be responsible for his own actions, has little perspective on the relative importance of his problems. It's not surprising that he may succumb to feelings of helplessness and hopelessness at times. Strong parental support will aid teen-agers in developing self-reliance and cautious optimism.

Loneliness is another factor in teen-age suicides—and it may well be that suicides occur at a much higher rate among college students than among other teen-agers. College students who are away from home for the first time may miss the security of family and friends. They may feel unable to adjust to their new surroundings. By the time a teen-ager goes to college, a parent should know how sensitive he is and be prepared to maintain contact and support long-distance.

Impulsiveness is another cause of adolescent suicide, since teen-agers often react to situations without thinking through the consequences. Angered by a fight with a friend or a run-in with a parent, teen-agers have been known to swallow sleeping pills or drive recklessly just to get back at whoever has made them mad or thwarted their will.

The adolescents most at risk as suicide attempters are girls. They comprise about three-quarters of the attempters, but boys make up three-quarters of the completed suicides. Boys are most likely to use violent methods such as jumping from heights, hanging, and gunshots, and unfortunately under these circumstances there is little likelihood of saving the victim's life. Girls, on the other hand, tend to take drugs (typically sleeping pills) or to slash their wrists; in short, slow methods of dying which make saving them a distinct possibility in most cases.

But how can all this help you in protecting your adolescent child? If you know the situations and times in which these youngsters are most at risk, you can watch them more closely, try to avoid or control precipitating situations, be alert for the warning signals, and take steps to intervene or to secure expert professional help in time to prevent this tragedy.

THE CUES AND THE CLUES

T.S. Eliot wrote that "April is the cruellest month," and he was right, for April and early May are the peak times for suicides. The spring, in fact, seems to bring both depression and suicide to their annual peaks. Psychiatrists explain this by pointing out that the depressed person is tormented and made to feel even worse by the sharp contrast between the terribly painful, cold unhappiness inside him and the bright, cheerful bursting-forth of new life, the sunlight and warmth, of the spring. Autumn runs second to the spring in suicide rates. The dying of the flowers and the leaves that were the glory of the summer, the beginning of the dark and cold that will be winter, emphasize the bleakness and the emptiness inside the gloomy, unhappy depressed person.

Any situation that causes the adolescent to feel insecure, unwanted, alone, depressed, and friendless becomes dangerous. Such feelings can also arise as a result of separation, divorce, or death in the family, or because of a chronic problem such as an alcoholic parent. The reasons teen-agers themselves give for their suicide attempts include impulse, a quarrel with parents, a relative, or friends, depression, school difficulties, emotional upset, unwanted pregnancy, and trouble with the law.

Actually, the problems that ultimately lead to teen-age suicide go much deeper and have usually been present since early childhood. One often finds that these teen-agers have suffered with increasing isolation and unhappiness, steadily decreasing self-esteem, and mounting depression. Physical illness, troubles at school, a shattered romance, an unexpected pregnancy—any of these can push the adolescent (normally none too secure at the best of times) over the edge. Teen-agers are particularly vulnerable if they have no confidant or role model. Death may seem the only way out of what appears to a teen-ager to be a hopeless impasse, an intolerable situation.

One of the most dangerous errors parents can make is to believe the old myth that those who threaten suicide or talk about it won't go through with it. In actual fact it's been shown that some three-quarters of suicides actually stated their intentions in advance. A story in a magazine of the American Medical Association told of a sixteen-year-old boy who argued sharply with his father over his grades in school and the use of the family car. Threatening to kill himself, he climbed up on the roof and moved listlessly to the edge. A crowd gathered in the street and someone derisively sneered, "Go ahead and jump!" The boy promptly leaped to his death. Where there is any danger or threat of suicide, a life is at stake. Don't hesitate: always get prompt, expert professional help.

Any suicide threat must be taken seriously, even if it is in a diary or a letter, or if it sounds vague, like "I wish it were all over . . . it's too much for me to take."

Many teen-agers won't talk about their contemplated suicide, but their actions will speak louder than words to a perceptive observer. Any abrupt changes either in behavior or personality must be regarded with suspicion and carefully evaluated. Unprovoked agitation, anxiety, or insomnia, loss of appetite, temper tantrums, or irritability are all danger signals. Frequent mood changes are indicative of a problem, as is the teen-ager's discarding something that he owns and previously has considered important to him. Of course, any attempts to obtain potential weapons or poisons that can be used for self-destruction are a sure indicator.

WHERE YOU CAN GET HELP

After a suicide attempt has been made, or if you suspect one might be made, you must obtain professional help, which is available from several sources. The best place to start might be with the teen-ager's own doctor. Most adolescent physicians are trained to know how to handle such a vital and delicate problem. However, you must feel sure that the doctor is a sensitive person who has a good working relationship with your teen-ager. A doctor should know if he can deal with the problem himself and provide enough help so that the teen-ager can cope adequately both with whatever triggered the particular episode and with the underlying, long-standing problems involved.

He also knows whether more specialized help is needed. He can recommend and refer the teen-ager to someone who is particularly interested and trained in both adolescent and suicide problems. This may be a psychiatrist or psychologist (often a suicidologist). Unfortunately, the high hopes once held for the suicide prevention centers and their hotlines have proven a disappointment, and NIMH no longer even supports them.

Unfortunately, the taboos about suicide lead parents to deny or conceal the suicide of a child. Physicians are also caught up in this taboo and prefer to label such happenings "accidental" whenever they can. This would cause no harm were it not for the fact that the surviving family and loved ones are severely damaged by such denials.

Ordinarily, grief and bereavement are normal processes that resolve themselves with patience and understanding. When suicide occurs—and it doesn't matter whether it's that of a child or an adult—the survivor can become the victim as well. For anger, rage, guilt, and shame all combine in overwhelming fashion to trigger a riot of thoughts, long-repressed memories, and bizarre wishes. Parents may develop an obsession with thoughts of how the death might have been prevented, how they failed to rescue the suicidal child—and this recrimination all too often results in self-flagellation or the blaming of others.

Out of all guilt comes an overwhelming hostility toward even such neutral figures as medical examiners, physicians, and hospital personnel. Mental health experts agree that immediate professional help is essential if the survivors in the family are to be saved—from feelings of remorse or from divorce, which is a frequent consequence.

Immediate psychiatric or psychological help should be sought and psychotherapy utilized to help parents reorganize themselves and their lives, and to save any surviving children. Highly skilled help is called for in this situation.

Fifteen

PROBLEMS OF BEREAVEMENT

NOTHING can be quite so painful to the adolescent as the tragic situations in which death strikes home, for youngsters are peculiarly sensitive to outside events and influences. Parents must carry a double burden here too, for while they strive to cope with their own traumatic and agonizing loss, they must simultaneously support and help their teen-ager to deal with death and loss, chronic illness, or physical disability. Divorces also take their toll on teen-ager and parent alike. Once more, the parent needs understanding, insight, and knowledge to deal constructively with these problems, but it is possible to teach a young person how to gain emotionally from his very losses, how to grow with grief.

Essentially we will be dealing here with the fundamental and universal issues of life that your youngster must learn for the rest of his or her life.

SEPARATION, LOSS, AND GRIEF

Birth itself is the first separation each of us experiences—a traumatic incident that psychiatrists see as a sort of psychological prototype, an experience full of emotional pain that will inevitably be reactivated and stirred up whenever any separation or loss occurs later in life. The fetus—living in a sheltered environment in the womb, guarded from abrupt changes or stimuli—is suddenly thrust forth at birth into a bright, noisy world with lower temperatures, chilling breezes, feels and touches, smells and tastes. Following the forced trip through the birth canal a riot of sensations and impulses is let loose upon the delicate new creature, and the infant's first cry may really be a protest against the trauma of this initial separation. From this point on, any of life's numerous separations will produce anxiety (so-called "separation anxiety") in both child and adult.

Separation occurs when the infant gives up the breast, when he learns to walk by himself. There is the separation of school for the first time (for both mother and child), and the cutting of ties as the child grows into the adolescent and then into the adult. But there can be no growth without separation, loss, and change, all of which go together.

In adolescence the child must achieve final separation from both childhood and parents, gain his independence, and grow into an adult. Parental help, support, and encouragement make this possible, and keep the trauma, turmoil, and pain of this period to a minimum as the teen-ager struggles with his separation anxieties. Conflict and turmoil increase, and tension rises, until finally the adolescent stands forth free and alone. With this achievement of independent adulthood comes tranquility and sureness—and a warm lifelong relationship with the parents who have helped.

The ability to gain and to grow from emotional losses is the most lasting gift the parent can give a teen-ager—for it will carry him or her through comfortably to the very end of life. How the parent grows and changes can provide support and encouragement for the youngster to do the same in the frightening passage through adolescence. It can help him try new and healthy changes of life-style, think and test and question rationally, and prepare himself for a lifetime of successful, continuing growth and happiness.

The death of a loved one or of any meaningful figure (President John F. Kennedy's death struck teen-agers particularly hard, for example) is the ultimate form of separation and loss. Bereavement or grief with its separation anxiety occurs with such a loss, or even when someone close goes on a trip or moves away. The French put it well when they say that every farewell is a little death. How then can parents handle this terrible tragedy for their youngster?

DEATH OF A PARENT

The adult who loses a parent goes through what Freud called "grief work," a very normal process. Grief is like a wound—if it's clean and healthy it will heal naturally over a period of time, although the process may be slow and painful. In healthy bereavement there is rethinking and refeeling, repeatedly remembering and reliving thoughts and feelings and memories revolving about the deceased, until over a period of months or years the pain, guilt, and anger that normally accompany grief, the anguish of loss and separation, all are slowly brought under control until they finally fade. The survivor who does this grief work well will emerge a richer, deeper, more compassionate human being.

But note the word "adult" that we carefully used here. Such mourning can only be successfully carried out by the person who has himself completed his own separation from his parents during adolescence. Psychiatrists now recognize that such mourning is only possible after the adolescent has at least reached the age of eighteen, when he or she should have completed separation from the parent. However, with the highly individual teen-age patterns, this age is variable.

It's vital for the parent to understand all this in order to deal successfully with the teen-ager who loses a parent. With this knowledge, the remaining parent can be of greater help to the suffering youngster and also avoid being hurt by the teen-age reaction, which may, by adult standards, seem heartless and even cruel. By knowing normal adolescent grief reactions, the parent can also tell when professional help is needed, so there will be no serious or permanent emotional damage.

Some experts believe that the child by the age of ten or eleven has virtually the adult understanding of the permanence of death. Teaching about death should start in the child's first years with explanations of dead insects or birds or pets. Acceptance of death often comes when a grand-parent or family friend, even a pet, dies. Honest, open discussion by parents is needed here, and parents should be clear in their own minds and feelings about the meaning of death and be able to express it frankly.

This is not nearly as simple as it sounds, for in our society there is a strong tendency to fear and to deny death—which is why people speak not of dying but of "passing away." It is to be hoped that we will soon return to the honesty about death that was present in earlier centuries when death was accepted as a real part of life, expressed in that ancient nursery rhyme:

> Doctor, Doctor, will I die?
> Yes, my child, and so shall I.

At each stage of the psychological development of the child there is a different kind of grief, a different way in which the child grieves for any separation or loss suffered. Should a parent die, the child will stop developing in the area of object relations, and the personal relationships of many of these children as they mature will remain shallow and inhibited all the rest of their lives. The child's ability to cope with this separation—the loss of a parent—depends on age. In general, the older the child the more developed his or her personality and psyche, the greater both the child's independence of the parent and the youngster's ability to cope.

The adolescent in general reacts to stress by reverting to a more childish level, by turning to the parents for the comfort and protection received as a child. The death of a parent compounds and worsens this situation, because in a very real sense the teen-ager finds he has lost not one but both parents, at least for a while—for the surviving parent is often depressed and no longer able to supply either the love or the support normally given.

Children under eighteen will be most damaged by such a tragic loss. Their confusion, conflict, and turmoil at this time, the repeated clashes and the attacks on the parent with the resultant guilt feelings, all leave the adolescent especially susceptible to feelings of remorse when a parent dies. In grief, the most damaging effects arise from any ambivalent feelings and unresolved anger felt by the survivor before the death. The resulting guilt produces a variety of unfortunate reactions, which prevent successful grief and leave problems that can persist for many years, even indefinitely, until psychotherapy clears the way for normal grief.

Teen-agers normally feel anger and ambivalence toward parents, and so when a youngster loses a parent he not only feels both the loss of that parent and of protection in this still-dependent stage of life, but he also feels the guilt now aroused by his behavior toward that now-dead parent. This may well lead the youngster even to deny the death.

Typical was a fourteen-year-old boy who, on the morning of the day his father was killed in an accident, had told him how much he hated him and everything he stood for. Yet at his father's funeral the youngster was telling visitors what a perfect father he had (he used the present tense, a denial of the death) even though those attending knew the father had not been effective as a parent and was often away on business. This same boy's mother felt hurt and startled a few weeks after the father's death to hear the boy telling family friends how fine things were and how much he was enjoying school and social activities. Actually the boy wasn't getting any of the joys or satisfactions he was proclaiming so loudly.

Adolescents under eighteen (those still tied to parents) often show only a seemingly short and very fleeting sadness, simply because they are not capable of carrying the heavy burden of adult grief. They seek protective escape in a surface happy-go-lucky attitude. The carefully listening parent can recognize this, for the suffering youngster will reveal his problems with his complaints: typically, a lack of energy, difficulties in falling asleep, loss of appetite, even an incapacity to "get with it." Careful observation will reveal that these youngsters are actually finding very little joy in their school or social lives, and have lost all interest in their pursuits and friends.

Typically, too, the bereaved adolescent may seek a substitute for the lost parent in a close relationship with a family friend or relation. The youngster may even feign worry about some minor complaint (a skin rash or muscle ache) as an excuse to visit the doctor, an authority figure and an ideal parent substitute, so a sensitive, knowledgeable physician can help here. In fact, along with doctors, members of the clergy, teachers, and youth leaders are all similar authority or parental figures to whom bereaved youngsters often and repeatedly turn.

The surviving parent must deal not only with his or her own grief but also be alert to the youngster's reactions and recognize them for what they actually are. The teen-ager's reduced capacity to enjoy or engage in his usual activities may last for several months. He may deny the relationship of such changes to the parent's death, simply because the subject is too painful for his still-immature mind to openly cope with.

Behavioral changes often result, ranging from not turning in school assignments to cutting classes, even to stealing (an expression of the anger felt at the loss and an attempt to get back the love that has been taken away). One fifteen-year-old girl would suddenly burst into tears over a seemingly totally unrelated event she read about or saw on TV, because it was safer and less painful for her to express her feelings that way, where it would not be too overwhelming. Any open, direct expression of this girl's feelings might have set off outright panic by forcing her to admit the death of her mother, an event she had been trying to deny and repress.

Too close an attachment between adolescent and surviving parent—especially one of the opposite sex—must be avoided, for it may actually hinder the youngster's working out the normal grieving. It's quite common in the immediate mourning period for parent and teen-ager to room or even sleep in the same bed, but this must be handled with care and not allowed to go on for more than a matter of days, perhaps a week or two. Extending such an arrangement into months is all too likely to prevent healthy grieving and completion of grief work by both parent and child alike.

Some expert advice may be immensely valuable. A competent, sensitive adolescent physician is likely to be the first source of help, although more specialized help (an adolescent psychiatrist, say) may be warranted. When behavioral or other changes continue in the youngster for weeks without signs of return to normalcy, professional consultation is called for. An unnecessary consultation will do no damage, but failure to secure a necessary one will. Expert advice may well prevent serious, permanent damage to the developing, highly sensitive teen-ager.

DEATH OF A SIBLING

Here too we have the same question of adult and childlike mourning. Eighteen year olds will usually carry out adult mourning, while younger teen-agers will show the different kind of grieving already described. However, teen-agers who lose a brother or sister will have the advantage of starting from an improved base, for both parents will be alive and capable of limited but still effective support.

Normal sibling rivalry with its competitiveness, envy, and hostility may create guilt. The greater the ambivalence and anger, the greater the guilt, and the more stormy and difficult course the grieving will take. Also, should there have been a period of prolonged illness, the healthy surviving child will have felt shut out and less loved because of the extra attention given to the sick sibling. The healthy child normally can be expected to have wished at times secretly or out loud that the sick sibling would hurry up and die. This leads to considerable guilt and terror.

Parents are left with a triple task—to carry out and deal with their own grief (the loss of a child is the most difficult bereavement to bear) while helping the surviving child to deal with his mourning. Finally, they must work to keep the family together and moving along in the essential ongoing business of living. All the problems of resolving the grief over a parent's death are present here, aggravated not only by the already mentioned special complications, but also by the surviving youngster's natural concern over his own personal death. Siblings tend to be similar ages, whereas parents seem very old to teen-agers and a sibling's death brings the fear of death all the closer.

Professional help is of great value here, for normal family life must be re-established under the most difficult of conditions. In particular, the parents must avoid the very common reaction of pressing the surviving child to compensate for the lost one by saying, "You're the oldest now" or "You must be as good in school as your sister was." There must be great understanding for the surviving teen-ager in his attempts to deny his loss, even though these may well make things doubly hard on the parents. One thirteen year old promptly asked for his dead brother's sports equipment, and a fifteen year old bitterly complained that the funeral interfered with her party plans. At such times, the parents must make an enormous effort not to berate their child for insensitivity.

Parents must also be very alert for any signs of the surviving sibling's failure to recover from grief and the reactions we've mentioned. If a child is slow to accept the loss, prompt professional help should be sought. Counseling might be utilized right from the start, for it may prevent difficulties and make the normal, healthy resolution of a crisis less traumatic.

Parents who lose a mate must deal with the grief openly and honestly, and the teen-ager (in spite of his denial or self-protective, often glib remarks) will respect his parent's sincere grief. Honesty in feelings is the surest way to gain an adolescent's respect and admiration.

Parents may never get over the loss of a child. It's the most "unnatural" of all deaths, an offense against nature, and a shock to parents, siblings, relatives, and friends. Almost three-quarters of marriages are said to end in separation after such a death. Sudden deaths are too intensely damaging. In fact, violent deaths—particularly suicide—call for prompt psychiatric intervention for parents and siblings. The family must be completely reconstituted, new relationships worked out, and expectations revised. One husband and wife who lost a fourteen year old in an accident became virtual strangers to each other and couldn't communicate their feelings for nearly a year afterward. They only began to talk to each other after intensive psychotherapy. It was more than a year before they could talk about their lost child and begin to think and plan as a family unit once more.

Reactions to grief are so strange and powerful that the sufferers seldom realize that their grief is neither a unique nor a disturbed reaction. Grief is normal. Numbness (nature's protective mechanism to keep the sufferer from a psychic shock that cannot be dealt with immediately) is not an uncommon feeling for the mourner who can neither realize nor accept the fact of death for a week or more. Recovery is slow, and bizarre reactions such as hallucinations are common. Physical reactions, such as a weight on the chest, difficulty in breathing, symptoms of various illnesses, are common, as is depression mixed with disturbances of the usual sleep patterns, either complete loss of appetite or an inability to stop eating, and a whole host of other psychosomatic symptoms. Strong mood and thought changes—anger, weeping, feelings of guilt, loss of memory—come and go almost uncontrollably. Time alone— one, two, three years—allows the pain to dull and lessen; but grief never wholly disappears in parents whose adolescent child has died.

Another difficult situation is the adolescent who is dying and whose parents must face the fact of, say, incurable cancer. Here, parents go through "anticipatory grief," with all the grief reactions but to a somewhat lesser extent. When the fatal disease takes one or more years to reach its conclusion, the parents may be almost without tears or any severe reaction by the time the end actually comes—not because they don't feel, but simply because much of the most acute grief has already been gone through. But the work of mourning will continue and the grief will last virtually without end.

One of the most difficult tasks for those parents who lose children is to keep the family together and protect any remaining siblings from the damage done by such tragedies. Professional help is extremely important in light of the high rate of marital break-ups at these times, and the terribly painful and lasting effects of such losses.

DIVORCE

Divorce entails another of life's major separations. Parents can anticipate a teen-ager's reacting essentially the same as to death but on a somewhat lesser scale, depending on how the explanation is handled. With the divorce rate approaching 40 percent, parents are becoming more sensitive to the responses of teen-agers in this situation. Children tend to see their parents as separating from *them* rather than from each other, and this causes great anguish.

Unfortunately, many parents may wait to divorce until their children are adolescents. Yet that is actually one of the most devastating ages for children to face divorce. Since teen-agers are themselves in the midst of rejecting their parents, a badly handled divorce could make this rejection permanent. It could even delay the teen-ager's maturation in some instances. With so much turmoil and disruption in his environment, an adolescent's growth can suffer a setback.

To minimize damage to the teen-ager, divorced parents should try to maintain the same personal relationships with their children and to be together at important events such as graduations and weddings.

When one is dealing with the emotional problems of teen-agers, professional help is always valuable, because the emotional nature of adolescent behavior makes it very difficult for the nonexpert and personally involved and concerned parent to evaluate objectively all the manifestations and indications that show themselves.

THE CHRONICALLY ILL OR DISABLED ADOLESCENT

Adolescents are very concerned with their own bodies— their "self-image." They are acutely disturbed at being different from peers, and they tend to be extremely active physically. If their bodies are interfered with by a sudden severe handicap at this crucial time of self-esteem, the result can be devastating.

The goal of adolescence is ultimately to achieve maturation and adulthood. But since most adolescents aim to be popular, the disabled or chronically ill teen-ager finds himself struggling with the virtually impossible task of seeking both acceptance and popularity among an extremely critical and frequently rejecting peer group. And he must do it with below-average resources or even marked handicaps.

At the very time the adolescent is striving to become independent, the unfortunate teen-ager with a chronic illness such as diabetes or arthritis not only finds his freedom limited physically, but he is placed in a position where he must accept strict medical orders and regimens (the equivalent of parental authority). The result is often a health disaster, because teen-age patients are extremely difficult to manage adequately as they battle necessary medical regimens such as diet, medication, and physical limitations. Teen-agers often get into serious and even life-threatening medical crises as a result of their rejection of authority and their attempts to be like their peers.

Parental overprotection poses another problem. It is often wise to learn all the medical details about your child's care and the extent of his capabilities. Psychological counseling can help for parents and teen-agers alike because of the problems encountered in this mercurial situation. Obviously, every effort must be made to help the chronically ill or disabled youngster to mature and to reach his fullest capacity, while recognizing and accepting the realistic limitations that illness or disability must of necessity impose.

Parents of infants born with significant congenital or inherited abnormalities (anything from mongolism to cleft palate) never cease to lament the lost "normality" of such children. The same reactions can be found when these disturbances first arise in adolescence. The reaction is similar to grief: denial and disbelief and a search for a physician who will tell them it isn't so. Negative reactions to deformed children may cause guilt feelings even though these reactions are normal. Such guilt feelings may in turn lead to overreaction and cause excessive protection of the child to the extent that he never gets a chance to mature or break free of his handicap. Again, professional help at a variety of levels, as we have already discussed, may prove immensely productive and valuable for both parents and teen-agers.

Sixteen

A FINAL WORD

EVERY teen-ager should have a "well examination" every year or year and a half, since adolescence is a critical period in life. Besides the usual complete physical examination to check all the tissues and organs doctors can see, probe, or hear, the checkup should include a urine analysis and blood tests (at the very least a hemoglobin check) plus anything that your youngster may individually need. We have already discussed the necessary immunizations young people require, but we want to recommend tuberculin testing every year from the age of thirteen to eighteen since the incidence of tuberculosis increases during those years, as explained earlier. Tragically, however, young people, because of embarrassment or rebelliousness or financial reasons, don't visit their personal doctor annually.

The importance of such well examinations goes far beyond the actual medical problems usually anticipated by parents in connection with such examinations. Take one youngster who came in for an injury and only then revealed his long-standing painful urination and "a drip" (which proved to be a serious infection). Were it not for the injury the infection would have been neglected even longer. An annual examination and a close relationship with his doctor developed over the years would have brought him in much sooner, before the infection could do serious damage.

The well examinations also give doctors the opportunity to explore their young patients' social lives, school activities, sports involvements, and sexual curiosity. Doctors can check their skin, discuss smoking, drugs, and sex, or whatever else is troubling the teen-age patient. Doctors might prevent many of the unnecessary and tragic problems we have discussed in this book.

To sum up adolescent health problems one must invariably come back to the fact that adolescence should be a healthy period, physically and medically, but it is not trouble-free by any stretch of the imagination. Emotional and psychological problems may exacerbate any medical disturbances that do arise. It is these difficulties that create the chief obstacles that physicians must overcome in treating the ailments (particularly such chronic ones as diabetes and arthritis) and in securing their patients' cooperation. An established and regular relationship certainly facilitates cooperation.

Besides the difficulty of getting a teen-ager to follow necessary medical regimens, the problems of how to persuade him to care for his own body properly, to accept regular medical checkups, and even to seek medical help when there is some specific ailment or problem are the great burden of the parent. The path lies in understanding the psychology of adolescents as presented here and in developing strong parent–child communication so that rational modern health measures can be taught and accepted.

Advising adolescents to follow a needed medical measure invariably runs afoul of their natural rebelliousness. An open, trusting relationship will often help the teen-ager comply with doctor's orders. A teen-ager's need to deny physical ailments or disabilities makes medical care difficult. There is no magic formula or pattern to be followed— each child is unique, and sensitive parents can only use whatever methods they find work best. Setting an example of a healthy life-style and a calm, rational approach to problems will benefit teen-agers most. Knowledgeable, understanding, and loving parents, and a concerned physician, will find their own way to the necessary medical care for the teen-ager despite all the problems. We hope that this book will provide you with the tools you need to help when it is needed.

FURTHER READING

"Alcohol and Health." Current Special Report to the U.S. Congress.

Anthony, E. J. "Between Yes and No: The Potentially Neutral Area Where the Adolescent and His Therapist Can Meet." Peter Blos Lecture, 1973.

Blotcky, M. "Adolescence." *Journal of the American Medical Association*, May 16, 1977.

Burchenal, J. H., and Burchenal, J. R. "Chemotherapy of Cancer." *Chemistry*, July/August 1977.

"Cigarette Smoking among Teen-Agers and Young Women." Public Health Service pamphlet, 1977.

Cutright, P. "The Teenage Sexual Revolution and the Myth of an Abstinent Past." *Family Planning Perspectives*, January 1972.

Dalton, K. *The Menstrual Cycle*. New York: Pantheon Books, 1969.

Daniel, W. A. *The Adolescent Patient*. St. Louis, Mo.: C. V. Mosby, 1970.

"Facts about Adolescence." National Institutes of Mental Health, 1974.

Farnsworth, D. *Psychiatry, Education and the Young Adult.* Springfield, Ill.: C. C. Thomas, 1966.

Freese, A. S. *Help for Your Grief*. New York: Schocken, 1977.

———. *The Miracle of Vision*. New York: Harper & Row, 1977.

———. *You and Your Hearing*. New York: Scribners, 1979.

Gallagher, J. R.; Heald, F. P.; and Garell, D. C., eds. *Medical Care of the Adolescent*, 3rd ed. New York: Appleton-Century-Crofts, 1976.

206   THE HEALTHY ADOLESCENT

Gianturco, D. T., and Smith, H. L. *The Promiscuous Teenager.* Springfield, Mass.: C. C. Thomas, 1966.
Gould, L. C., et al. "Sequential Patterns of Multiple-Drug Use among High School Students." *Archives of General Psychiatry,* February 1977.
Greep, R. O., et al. *Reproduction and Human Welfare.* Cambridge, Mass.: M.I.T. Press, 1976.
Halleck, S. L. "Why Adults Hate Kids." *Think,* November-December 1970.
Kantner, J. F., and Zelnik, M. "Sexual Experience of Young Unmarried Women in the United States." *Family Planning Perspectives,* October 1972.
Kolb, L. C. *Modern Clinical Psychiatry,* 8th ed. Philadelphia: Saunders, 1973.
Lester, D. "Prevention of Suicide." *Journal of the American Medical Association,* August 20, 1973.
Lettieri, D. J., ed. *Predicting Adolescent Drug Abuse.* . . . Rockville, Md.: National Institute on Drug Abuse, 1975.
Levy, E. Z. "Some Thoughts on Adolescence." *Menninger Perspective,* Fall 1973.
McDonald, T. F. "Teenage Pregnancy." *Journal of the American Medical Association,* August 9, 1976.
"Marihuana and Health." Sixth Annual Report to the U.S. Congress, 1976.
Modlin, H. C. "Society and Drugs." *Menninger Perspective,* Summer 1974.
Pinkel, D. "Curability of Childhood Cancer." *Journal of the American Medical Association,* March 8, 1976.
Schowalter, J. E. "Parent Death and Child Bereavement" in *Bereavement* by Schoenberg et al. New York: Columbia University Press, 1975.
Seiden, R. H. "Suicide Capital? A Study of the San Francisco Suicide Rate." *Bulletin of Suicidology,* December 1967.
Shearin, R. B. "Contraception for Adolescents." *American Family Physician,* March 1976.
Spindler, E. B., and Acker, G. "Teen-Agers Tell Us about Their Nutrition." *Journal of the American Dietetic Association,* September 1963.
Stickle, G. "Pregnancy in Adolescents." *Contemporary Ob/Gyn,* June 1975.
"Suicide among Youth." Supplement to *Bulletin of Suicidology,* 1969.
Sulzberger, M. B. *Growth at Adolescence,* 2nd ed. Philadelphia: Lippincott, 1962.

Tanner, J. M. *Growth at Adolescence*, 2nd ed. Philadelphia: Lippincott, 1962.

Walters, P. A., et al. "Drug Use and Life-Style among 500 College Undergraduates." *Archives of General Psychiatry*, January 1972.

Winder, A. E. *Adolescence: Contemporary Studies*, 2nd ed. New York: D. Van Nostrand, 1974.

Youngs, D. D., and Niebyl, J. R. "Adolescent Pregnancy and Abortion." *Medical Clinics of North America*, November 1975.

Index

abortion
  vs. adoption, 67–68
  professional counseling in, 69
acne, 150–54
acting-out behavior, 17–18
acute lymphatic leukemia (ALL),
  119–20
adolescence
  child abuse in, 31–32
  defined, 5–6
  early, 9–13
  goals of, 10–11, 13, 15, 19
  growth patterns in, 38–39,
    43–47
  abnormal, 51–55
  growth rate in, 12–13, 40–43
  late, 14–16
  medical checkups in, 202–3
  medical disorders in, 203–4. *See*
    also specific name
  middle, 13–14
  parental relations in. *See*

  parent-adolescent relations
  period of, 5–6
  physical disabilities in, 199–201
  sexual maturation in, 6, 10,
    11–12, 39–40, 48–51
  medical problems of, 150–64
  view of parents in, 32–35
  See also specific subject
adolescent behavior, 3–5, 8, 14
  identity crisis and, 8–9, 15–16
  maladjusted, 17–18
  incidence of, 167–68
  recovery from, 174–75
  treatment of, 172–74
  warning signals for, 165–66,
    168–72
  normal, 166–67
  after parental death, 188–94
  peer influence on, 16–17, 27
  after sibling death, 194–98
  See also sexual behavior
adoption, *vs.* abortion, 67–68